PSYCHOLOGY: EXPERIMENTS, INVESTIGATIONS AND PRACTICALS

Mark Lisney

Blackwell Education

Thanks to Jo for the loan of the shampoo . . .

© Mark Lisney 1989
First published 1989

Design and illustration © Basil Blackwell Ltd

Published by
Basil Blackwell Ltd
108 Cowley Road
Oxford OX4 1JF
England

British Library Cataloguing in Publication Data

Lisney, Mark
 Psychology: experiments, investigations & practicals
 1. Psychology. Experiments
 I. Title
 150'.724

 ISBN 0–631–90349–6

Cover: Bridget Riley, 'Movement in Squares' tempera on board, 48" × 48", 1961
     Courtesy of the Mayor Rowan Gallery

Typeset in 11/13 Palatino by
Wearside Tradespools, Fulwell, Sunderland
Printed in Great Britain by Dotesios (Printers) Ltd., Trowbridge, Wilts.

Contents

Foreword

To the teacher

The material in this book has been written in a way that allows for flexible use. When referring to lower level courses I mean GCSE. Higher level courses refer to GCE A and A/S level, BTec National Diploma and Scottish Higher level.

Section One

This section consists of structured student material that can be used in a number of different ways. Each exercise should take 10 to 20 minutes to complete, depending on the ability of the student.

The Shampoo Conspiracy uses the everyday example of washing hair as a vehicle for introducing the basic concepts in experimental design and statistics. Even low ability groups are able to relate to this example and make competent suggestions about what would need to be done to test the idea that shampoos contain a tangling agent. Before writing these materials, I used the example as a discussion exercise and found that many students could point out potential independent variables such as hair types, and suggest the need for a large sample.

It is well known that students' learning is facilitated by everyday examples that they can relate to. I have tried to play on that theme, and I suspect that the storyline helps to keep the attention of, and organise the memories of, the less able students. The examples are obviously not psychological in content; I would suggest that what is important is to teach the basic concepts in the simplest way possible and then to relate these to examples from psychology.

For lower level courses the material included should be sufficient to cover course requirements. For higher level courses the material aims to supplement existing textbooks on experimental design and

1

statistics and to provide an active learning experience to back up a textbook. The material could reasonably be used for the first part/year of a higher level course, to ensure that students learn the basics before they are given a more advanced book.

Wherever possible I have tried to structure the material in a way that encourages the student to actively think about the information. Obviously, trying to find a middle path between the ability range found in lower level groups and those found in higher level courses has been difficult.

I have found the most effective way to use the material is to get each student to attempt each exercise individually, and then go over the answers as a group. This allows each student both to benefit from working on their own, and to gain from the input of other members of the class. It also allows for individual problems with concepts to be identified and dealt with individually.

The material can equally act as small units of homework assigned at the end of each lesson, and then either handed in or answered as a group at the beginning of the next lesson. (This may be more suitable for evening classes where class time is extremely limited, and the students are self motivated.)

Presented opposite are examples of how the materials might be used for lower and higher level courses. The concepts covered are based on an analysis of GCSE syllabuses (lower level courses) and 'A' level, BTec National and Highers (higher level courses). You should, of course, check the specific coverage of the syllabus you are following.

LOWER LEVEL COURSES

You may feel that the content suggested is somewhat ambitious for some lower level courses, as it leads up to a basic understanding of significance. It is my experience, however, that the presentation of these ideas via dialogue and playing on commonsense knowledge makes this feasible even with lower ability students.

The material in this section aims to introduce some of the major methods of investigation in psychology, and to point out some of the major advantages and disadvantages of the methods. This is a common component of both GCSE and 'A' level syllabi. The advantages and disadvantages offered will probably be sufficient for GCSE course requirements, but at 'A' level the material will act as an introduction.

Each method is briefly described and its main advantages are given. This is then followed by an example of the application of the method and a structured question. All examples present evidence that is relevant to the continuing debate over the effects of violent TV. This topic area was chosen as it usually arouses interest in students and is frequently included in examination syllabi.

To encourage students to be analytical about the evidence that is presented, I ask them to role play the characters on either side of the 'Violence on TV' debate. Although some might argue that encouraging students to take sides in a polarised debate narrows their conception of the complexity of the issues, I feel that the exercise helps them be more critical of the evidence presented and is thus a useful first step in encouraging analysis.

Students are encouraged to see how many sources of evidence can throw light on a particular problem, and how a single source of evidence can give rise to many opposing viewpoints. The material aims to help build up the skills necessary for 'discussing' a topic in an essay. This is a complex skill and many students find it a difficult one to acquire. For 'A' level students the material could be usefully followed up with an essay title that asks them to discuss the evidence that TV violence is a cause of aggression.

The summary table on page 200, can be used in different ways. For GCSE candidates it could form a running summary that they fill in as they look at each new method of investigation. More able students could be asked to complete the table as a test.

(One notable omission from this section is the survey method. This would need to be covered separately.)

5

Section Three

The practicals in this section have been selected with the following criteria in mind:

1 They report papers written in the 1980s.
2 They can be carried out with the minimum of equipment – using items normally found in a Further Education College (eg a photocopier, card, telephone, Yellow pages and in one case video equipment).
3 They reflect a wide range of subject matter.
4 They can be carried out with minimal preparation.

All of the practicals include background material. This will help students in writing the introduction section of a report and in understanding the research background to the practical. Each practical has a list of *keywords* which can be used to find related information in other psychology texts. Some of the suggested variations to the practical consist simply of open questions which provide ideas for further investigation within introductory courses. This may constitute original research!

Most of the practicals could be attempted with lower level groups, as long as the simplest suggested method is chosen, and the analysis of results is kept to descriptive statistics. A few are more complex, and only suitable for higher level courses. These are: The Recency Effect and the Modality Effect; Belief in the Paranormal; Preference for Surnames; Memory for Pictorial Advertising. (Belief in the Paranormal requires a Likert scale to be constructed before the actual practical is carried out, and this would make it a fairly lengthy practical.)

The analysis suggestions for each practical have been kept to a minimum. This will be appropriate for more able students, but less able students will need more in-depth instruction.

In the Appendix of this section there are word lists and word squares with a brief explanation of their possible uses which could be developed into other practicals.

Warning. Some of the practicals are not suitable for use with subjects who have read this book. If subjects are aware of what is being tested and why, this may well influence the results.

To the student

This book is divided into three sections:

Section One *The Great Shampoo Conspiracy* aims to explain the basics of experimental design and statistics.

Section Two *Methods of investigation* explains the advantages and disadvantages of different forms of investigation used in psychology.

Section Three *Practicals* outlines and provides material for studies that can be carried out in introductory psychology courses.

Some advice. Do not attempt to cover too many of the topics at once. Leave yourself some time for the information to sink in. Before you do a new section, quickly re-read the last one that you did, to refresh your memory.

Section One

The material in this section can be used for two levels of courses. The lower level course should cover all that is required for GCSE. The higher level course will cover a substantial portion of what is required for GCE A and A/S level, BTec National Diploma and Scottish Higher courses.

Many students find the experimental method and statistics part of the course the hardest. This may be because the material forces you to think slowly and carefully. If you find a section difficult, read through it one or two sentences at a time. After each sentence, try to put it into your own words. If you still find it difficult, ask your teacher or another student to explain it, or look at another textbook. Sometimes all that is needed is for the material to be explained in a slightly different way.

Section Two

Section Two explains the advantages and disadvantages of the different forms of investigation used in psychology. This section aims to teach you to be critical of evidence that is presented in support of an argument.

One major method that is not covered in this book is the survey method, and you should try to find out about this method from other sources.

Section Three

Section Three contains practicals suitable for introductory courses in psychology. Each practical includes background information to give you an idea of the type of research that has been carried out on the topic. This background material is presented in concise note form. If you need to find out about any of the ideas of concepts mentioned, use the *keywords* listed. These will help you look up the topic in other psychology textbooks. This section is about active learning, practical work and up-to-date research – it does not aim to give you a lot of detailed information.

Beware. Some of the practicals are not suitable for use on people who have read this book and know what you are trying to test. When people know they are being studied they sometimes act differently and this distorts the results you would get from your study.

SECTION ONE
THE GREAT SHAMPOO
CONSPIRACY

1 The Great Shampoo Conspiracy
OR *How to tell if you're being conned by the adverts . . .*

The other day I found that I had run out of shampoo. I decided that I would borrow some from my flatmate. The shampoo that I borrowed was one of those posh shampoos that is meant to be used with a conditioner. After I had washed my hair with this shampoo, I noticed that my hair seemed a lot more tangled than it did after washing with my normal shampoo.

Why should this be?

- Could it be that the shampoo was not for my hair-type?

- Could it be that I hadn't washed my hair as thoroughly as I normally did?

- Could it be that I was more observant of the effects of this shampoo, because it was new?

- Or . . . could it be that the manufacturers had deliberately put a chemical into the shampoo to tangle up my hair so that I then had to buy the conditioner?

I decided that the last explanation was the most likely to be right. The new shampoo was for normal hair, and so was my old shampoo. I felt that I had probably washed my hair as thoroughly as usual, and I was fairly sure that my hair was more tangled than normal. But these were just feelings. I needed proof. I needed to *test out* my ideas.

The next day I went to the shops and bought a range of shampoos from real cheapies to really upmarket, special, magic-ingredient shampoos. Each day I washed my hair for two minutes in a different shampoo, and dried it in the same way. For each shampoo I kept a

11

record of how many times I had to run the comb through my hair to make it tangle free. The results seemed to suggest that I was right in suspecting a conspiracy. Generally, the more expensive the shampoo the more times I had to comb my hair to make it tangle free.

Table 1.1 shows my results.

Day	Cost of shampoo (per 100 ml)	Number of combings
1	35p	5
2	£1.26	18
3	£1.17	17
4	£1.02	14
5	76p	11
6	54p	15
7	47p	10
8	23p	3

Table 1.1

Questions

Note It is important to answer the questions. Sometimes questions introduce new ideas, but usually they help you check that you have understood the material in each section. If you do not answer the questions, you may encounter difficulties with later sections.

1 In psychology an idea that is to be tested is called a hypothesis. What was the hypothesis that I tested?

2 How did I test out my hypothesis?

3 Why did I make sure that I washed with each shampoo for two minutes?

4 Apart from the two minutes, what else should I have controlled for each shampoo (ie what else should I have kept the same?). Hint: there are a number of things that should have been kept constant.

5 What is the arithmetic mean of the number of combings. (To work out the arithmetic mean: add up all the scores, then divide the total by the number of scores.)

6 Copy Figure 1.1. Plot the number of combings against the price of the shampoo per 100ml.

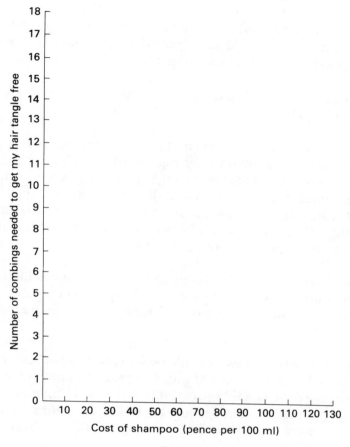

Fig 1.1

7 Which score goes against the general trend?

8 Does this study provide any evidence to support my hypothesis (see q.1)?

Elated by my discovery, I confidently told my flatmate that she was wasting her money, buying expensive shampoo. She immediately challenged me and asked me for evidence. I told her about the study, showed her my table of results, and sat back smugly.

Jo was not impressed. Not only was she annoyed that I had borrowed her shampoo in the first place, she also said my study proved nothing at all!

'First,' she said, 'your results only apply to your hair, so how can you tell me or anybody else that they are wasting their money? You can't generalise the results of your study to everybody else.'

'Second,' she continued, 'your study could have been affected by your own bias. You could have pulled harder with the comb after washing with the cheaper shampoos just to prove yourself right.'

'And finally,' she finished up, 'you have not kept everything constant for each test.'

Although Jo was rather annoyed at me for using her shampoo, and was not convinced by my testing of the hypothesis, she was interested. She agreed that there might just be a grain of truth in my idea. She suggested that we should design a better study before we started telling anyone else about it, or accusing shampoo companies of fiddling. After all, they might sue, and we needed a watertight case before we exposed them in the press.

First we discussed which shampoos to use. We decided that it would be much simpler, quicker and cheaper to compare just two shampoos. We would use my old shampoo and her more expensive shampoo.

Jo told me that a hypothesis should be worded in a particular way, ie such and such *will affect* something. The proper name for the first bit is the **independent variable** – the bit that the experimenter changes. The proper name for the second bit is the **dependent variable** – which is measured or recorded. So in our case the experimental hypothesis became:

The type of shampoo used to wash a person's hair	*will affect*	The number of combings needed to make hair tangle free.

Jo wasn't prepared to mess around with her hair for this study, so she volunteered my hair. (Thanks a lot, Jo!)

Jo suggested that the way to get rid of my bias was for me not to know which shampoo was being used. So we arranged that every morning at roughly the same time she would wash my hair with the same amount of either the cheap or the expensive shampoo for two minutes. I would then dry my hair in the normal way and count how many combings were needed to get my hair tangle free. She

14

also decided to toss a coin to decide which shampoo we would use each night, and to stop when we had an equal number of trials for each shampoo.

Other things that could affect the dependent variable, but which are not meant to be part of the study, are called **potential independent variables**. All of these need to be kept constant so that we can isolate the effect of the independent variables we are interested in. So in the shampoo experiment, by keeping potential independent variables constant we are controlling for their effects by making them the same for the expensive and cheap shampoos.

Jo said that the results of my first study could have been due to my bias (ie I could have tugged harder with the comb). In the study that Jo and I are doing together, we are controlling for my bias by not allowing me to know which shampoo is being used. This means when I take the measurements I will not be able to deliberately influence the results. Studies in which the subjects are either not told the true reason for doing the study, or are not informed of the changes that the experimenter is making are called single blind studies. (So our study is a single blind study.)

Double blind studies are ones in which both the experimenter and the subject are unaware of the changes being made.

Questions

1 What is the correct way to write a hypothesis?

2 In this study:
   a What was the independent variable?
   b What was the dependent variable?

3 In our experiment, which potential independent variables were controlled? State each one clearly and say how it was controlled.

4 What other potential independent variables could have been controlled? Name them and suggest ways of controlling them.

5 a Is there any way in which Jo's bias towards the expensive shampoo might allow her to influence the results?
   b How could our study be made into a double blind study?

After 20 nights Jo said it was time to stop and look at the results (Table 1.2).

Day	Type of shampoo	Number of combings	Day	Type of shampoo	Number of combings
1	Cheap	11	11	Cheap	10
2	Exp	13	12	Cheap	8
3	Exp	11	13	Cheap	9
4	Exp	12	14	Cheap	9
5	Exp	10	15	Exp	14
6	Cheap	7	16	Exp	11
7	Cheap	15	17	Cheap	7
8	Exp	11	18	Exp	11
9	Cheap	9	19	Cheap	10
10	Exp	9	20	Exp	12

Table 1.2

Jo said that we should use some descriptive statistics to summarise the raw data.

'Some what to do what to what?' I asked (sounding like a backing singer).

'Descriptive statistics are ways of summing up and describing the results,' Jo replied. 'What we have in the table is the raw data, and because there are ten scores for each shampoo it is difficult to see whether there are any overall differences.'

'So we have to cook the raw data with the statistics?'

'Yes, if you want to see it like that. The statistics are ways of mixing up all the raw data and getting a clearer view of the results. These are really simple statistics and all you have to do is follow the recipes.'

'Are you sure?'

'Positive. Look, I'll work out the stats for the cheap shampoo and you work them out for the expensive shampoo.'

1 *The arithmetic mean* is what most people mean when they talk about an average. It is obtained by adding up the scores and dividing by the number of scores. So for the cheap shampoo the scores are $11 + 7 + 15 + 9 + 10 + 8 + 9 + 9 + 7 + 10$ which makes a total of 95. There are ten scores so the total is divided by ten. $95 \div 10 = 9.5$. So the mean is 9.5.

16

2 *The mode* is another form of average. The mode is the most frequent score. For the cheap shampoo the score that occurs the most is 9. So the mode is 9.

3 *The median* is yet another form of average. The median is the middle score when data is placed in size order or, if there isn't a middle score, it is the midpoint of the two middle scores. To work it out you first put the scores in size order: so for the cheap shampoo: 7, 7, 8, 9, 9, 9, 10, 10, 11, 15, and then as we have two middle scores: 9 and 9, we add these together and divide by two: $9 + 9 = 18 \div 2 = 9$. So the median is 9.

The mean, mode and median are all measures of **central tendency**, ie they are all different ways of finding a central score in a set of scores. As well as describing a set of scores by stating what the average scores are, we can also describe them in terms of how spread out the scores are. The simplest measure of **spread** is the **range**.

To work out the range you subtract the lowest score from the highest score. So for the cheap shampoo the highest score is 15, and the lowest score is 7. $15 - 7 = 8$. So the range is 8.

Questions

1 Work out the mean, mode and median for the expensive shampoo and put them in a table like this:

	Mean	Mode	Median
Cheap shampoo	9.5	9	9
Expensive shampoo			

Table 1.3 Table of averages

2 Work out the range for the expensive shampoo.

3 Another form of descriptive statistics is graphs. Figure1.2 is a **histogram** of the frequency distribution for the scores of the cheap shampoo. I have also shaded the mode. Draw a similar graph for the expensive shampoo.

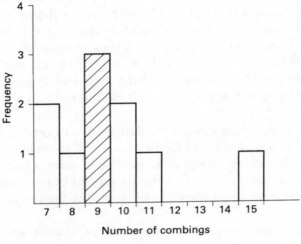

Fig 1.2

4 What evidence is there to suggest that the expensive shampoo caused more tangling than the cheap shampoo? Use the evidence (results and statistics) that are in this section.

5 Are there any odd or unusual results (ie results that go against the trend)?

I was over the moon as I thought that the results supported the hypothesis.

Jo said she wasn't so sure. 'Look, there is very little difference between the averages, and the highest number of combings occurred when we used the cheap shampoo.'

'But that was a freak result,' I protested.

'Maybe,' she replied, 'but it could be that it was the only true result and the other results were all freaks.'

'That's highly unlikely, isn't it?' I said.

'Yes, but there is a possibility that our results occurred by chance.'

'But you could say that about any set of results couldn't you?' I

18

replied. 'We could continue the study for 100 trials with each shampoo and although the results of almost all of the trials showed that the cheap shampoo was more effective, you could still say that. Even if we have 1000, or 10,000 trials you could still say that the results were due to chance, couldn't you?'

'That's why we need to use a statistical test,' said Jo. 'Any set of results could have been due to chance; that's why we need to find out what the possibility was that our results were due to chance.'

'Eh?' I said, confused.

'What I mean is, we have to use a test to find out if our results were probably due to the different shampoos we used, or whether they are the type of results that are likely to have happened by chance alone. Statisticians have designed tests that will tell you what the likelihood is of getting particular results by chance. In other words the test will tell you the **probability** of the results happening by chance.'

'How does that help us show which shampoo is better than the other.'

'Well, if we find that our results are very improbable, we can conclude that the difference we found between the cheap and the expensive shampoo is probably a real difference. Or, as they say in the trade, a **significant difference**. So we can then say that our hypothesis is probably correct.'

'Only probably correct?'

'Yes, because there is still a possibility that our results were due to chance, however small a possibility. With any set of results there is always this possibility ... The larger the difference is, the smaller the possibility that the results happened by chance, but there is still a possibility and this should not be forgotten.'

Questions

1 When you toss a coin there is as much of a chance that it will land with the head facing up, as with the tail facing up. In other words, the head and the tail are equally probable events. But this only holds true for coins that are properly weighted.

a *Problem:* I give you two coins and tell you that one of them is biased so that it is more likely to come up heads, and the other is an equally weighted coin. How many times would you need to toss each coin to find out which one was weighted?

b If you had done that would you be 100% sure that you had picked the right coin?

c If you were in the grips of a mad manic scientist who would kill you if you got the answer wrong, would it affect the number of times that you would want to toss the coins? How?

d If you increase the number of times that you toss the coins, what does this do to the chance that you might have the wrong answer? Does it increase the chance or decrease the chance?

2 A die has six sides and is numbered one to six. If you throw two dice:

a What is the most likely total score?

b What is the least likely score? Copy and complete Figure 1.3 to help you get the answers.

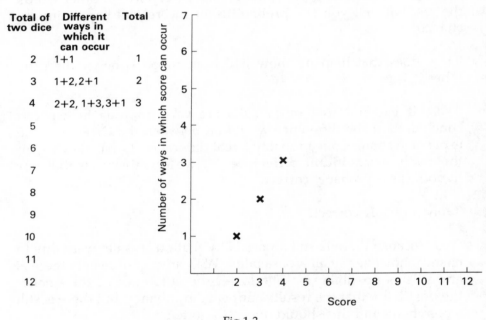

Total of two dice	Different ways in which it can occur	Total
2	1+1	1
3	1+2, 2+1	2
4	2+2, 1+3, 3+1	3
5		
6		
7		
8		
9		
10		
11		
12		

Fig 1.3

c What is the total number of outcomes, ie what is the total number of ways in which two dice can fall?

d With one die the likelihood of throwing a six is 1 in 6. (There is only one six on the die and there are six possible outcomes.) From the answer to **c**, what is the chance of throwing two sixes if you throw two dice?

'OK then Jo, if I have to know about these tests of significance it sounds as though I'm going to have to understand probability first. So I suppose you had better explain … and knowing you, you probably will,' I added.

'You already know the meaning of probability. You've just used the word in its everyday sense. You said that I "probably will" which means that I am likely to explain, or there is a good chance that I will explain.'

'OK that's obvious. But I'm sure that being maths, there will be millions of symbols and things.'

'Well no, not really, only a couple. Don't be scared of the symbols – they are only shorthand for very simple ideas. The first one is very simple. Instead of writing "probability" all the time statisticians just use the letter "p". The other two symbols are less than ($<$) and greater than ($>$). These signs are just arrowheads; the point always points to the smaller part of the equation.'

'Don't say that word …'

'Ahh don't be silly, these are simple ones. Anyway to get back to the main point: Probability is the likelihood or chance that something will happen. If something *always* happens it has a probability of one ($p = 1$). If something *never* happens it has the probability of zero ($p = 0$). Most of the time the extremes of zero and one are never used, and most of the time you talk about values between zero and one.'

'You mean that most probabilities are greater than zero ($p > 0$), or put the other way around, most probabilities are less than one ($p < 1$).'

'Good, you seem to have got the basics.'

'OK, but give me a couple of real-life examples.'

Jo wrote the following examples on a sheet of paper:

The probability of a coin landing head up is: $p = 0.5$

The probability of picking out a diamond card from a full set of cards is: $p = 0.25$

The probability of a person growing to 6 metres tall is: $p = 0$

The probability of winning the pools is: $p < 0.0000001$

I looked at the sheet and said 'Well the first three examples are OK, I can recognise those examples easily. For the coin I know that the chance of throwing a head is 1 in 2, and I can recognise 0.5 as a half (1/2). The card example is also OK, I know that there are four types of card in a pack, and 0.25 is the same as a quarter (1/4). Also I know it is impossible for a person to be 20ft high, but the last one is a bit confusing. I can see that the chance of winning the pools is less than a very small decimal, but I can't convert it into the idea of one in howevermany.'

Jo giggled.

'OK, what's so funny?'

With a more serious look on her face she said, 'I'm sorry. It's just that to have worked out the coins and the cards examples you must have subconsciously used one of the methods needed for the pools example. One way of doing it for decimals that are less than 0.5 is to divide 1 by the decimal. So for example, if you divide 1 by 0.5 you get 2, and if you divide 1 by 0.25 you get 4.

Division

Questions

1 Use the same method to work out the chance of winning the pools. Express it as: The chance of winning the pools is less than 1 in ... Use a calculator.

2 Look at this example:

$p < 0.1$ the probability is less than 1 in 10

Now work out the following: $p < 0.05$; $p < 0.002$; $p < 0.01$; $p < 0.001$.

Unfortunately this method only works for probabilities that are less than 0.5 (1 in 2). For probabilities greater than 0.5 ($p > 0.5$), an alternative method can be used. This is to subtract the probability from 1, work out what the remainder is in words, and then subtract this from 1.

For example, $p > 0.95$

Take 0.95 from 1, the remainder is 0.05, which is 1 in 20. One = 20 out of 20. Therefore: $p > 0.95$ means the probability is greater than 19 out of 20.

3 Use the above method to work out the following examples: $p < 0.99$; $p > 0.99$; $p > 0.9$; $p > 0.995$.

4 Another way to talk about probabilities is to talk about them as though they were percentages. So $p = 0.5$ is called a probability of 50%. A probability of $p = 0.1$ is a probability of 10%. This is simply worked out by moving the decimal point two places to the right. What are the following in percentages: $p = 0.05$; $p = 0.005$; $p = 0.9995$?

'Well I think I've mastered probability,' I said confidently, 'on with these significant differences.'

Jo explained again that the purpose of a test of difference was to work out the probability that a difference between two sets of scores occurred by chance.

'You see, we want to know if there has been an "experimental effect", that is, whether the independent variable affected the dependent variable.'

'You mean, in our case, if it was the type of shampoo that caused the difference in the number of combings until my hair was tangle free?'

'Exactly,' she agreed. 'We want to know whether we should accept or reject our null-hypothesis.'

'Our what?'

'Our null hypothesis. Whenever an experiment is carried out there is always an experimental hypothesis and a null hypothesis. The null hypothesis predicts that the independent variable will not affect the dependent variable. That is, it will not cause a difference in the number of combings.'

She wrote down the experimental and null hypothesis for our experiment:

Experimental: The type of shampoo will affect the number of combings needed.

Null: The type of shampoo will not cause a difference in the number of combings needed.

'You see,' she continued, 'the general aim of any experiment is to test the null hypothesis.'

'You mean prove it wrong.'

'Well, prove is a word that should be avoided. A better way of saying it is to say an experiment tries to falsify the null hypothesis.'

'So how does this test come into it?'

'The test processes the result in a way that allows us to decide whether the null hypothesis is likely to be correct.'

'And how does it do that?'

'The test works out how probable the difference found in the results is. Small differences between sets of scores are likely to occur by chance, but large differences are not. If the difference found is likely to have happened by chance the experimenter should accept the null hypothesis. If the difference is highly improbable the experimenter should reject the null hypothesis and accept the experimental hypothesis.'

How unlikely does the null hypothesis have to be before we can say that there is a significance difference?'

'Well, as a rule of thumb, if the probability that the null hypothesis is correct is less than (or equal to) 1 in 20 ($p < 0.05$), then we usually reject the null hypothesis and accept the experimental hypothesis. We can then say that our results are significant at the $p = 0.05$ level.'

Questions

1 I have an idea that the amount of alcohol a person consumes will affect their performance on a Space Invader machine.

   a What is the independent variable?
   b What is the dependent variable?
   c What would the null hypothesis be?

The 'rule of thumb' significance level of $p < 0.05$ is acceptable for almost all studies in the social sciences. If our results are significant at this level, then we can say that we have a greater than 19 out of 20 confidence level; or a confidence level of greater than 95%. This level of confidence is how sure we are that the hypothesis is correct.

On some occasions a $p < 0.05$ significance level is not enough to give scientists confidence in their results. This has to be the case if, say, people might suffer due to the use of incorrect findings. (For example, the results of tests on drugs.)

2 Work out the levels of significance for the following significance levels: $p < 0.1$; $p < 0.002$; $p < 0.0001$.

3 a What type of research do you think would need higher levels of confidence than 95%?
b Why do you think this needs higher levels of confidence?

4 If the independent variable affects the dependent variable, what is this called?

5 Copy the following paragraph and fill in the missing words:

The aim of any experiment is not to prove the hypothesis but to try to _____ the null hypothesis. If a test tells an experimenter that there is not a significant difference the experimenter must _____ the null hypothesis, but if there is a significant difference they must _____ the null hypothesis and _____ the experimental hypothesis.

The next day Jo came back from the library with a book of statistical tests. I thumbed through it warily.

'There seems to be lots of different types of tests in here,' I said, 'tests of difference . . . tests of correlation . . . tests of goodness of fit . . . which one do we need?'

'Well we carried out an experiment that predicted that there would be a difference, therefore we need a test of difference.'

'Yes, but which one? There are even different types of tests of difference. What does it mean when it talks about parametric and non-parametric tests?'

'That's a bit like the difference between a good quality stereo and the old-fashioned mono record players. The good quality record player is only suitable for records that are in good condition, ie the player "assumes" the records are not scratched, warped or covered in dirt. But the old mono players would play virtually any record, whatever its condition.'

'What's that got to do with these tests?'

'Parametric tests are a bit like the good quality record players. They are only suitable for high quality data. Before you use a parametric test you must test the data in a number of ways. Non-parametric tests are like the old mono players – they can be used with almost any set of data.'

'So how do you know if data is suitable for a parametric test?'

'Well if you had a record and you were deciding what player to play it on, you would probably go through a series of decisions. First you would see whether the record was mono or stereo, then you'd check to see if it was warped, and then look to see if it was scratched. Only if it passed all the tests would you play it on the good player.'

'But I can't see whether data is warped or scratched!'

'Of course not, but you can check whether the data is interval level of measurement, whether the samples have similar variance, and whether the samples are drawn from a normal distribution and are themselves relatively normally distributed.'

'Can I?'

'You will be able to soon. Parametric tests are used when the data is interval or ratio level, when the samples are normally distributed and when there is little or no difference between the variances of the samples. Non-parametric tests are used when any or all of the things are untrue.'

'If non-parametric tests can be used with almost any set of data, why bother with parametric tests?'

'Because parametric tests are more powerful. They have what is called greater power efficiency which means, in general terms, that they are able to detect significant differences from smaller actual differences in data.'

'So, in some circumstances, if you got a significant difference with a parametric test you would not get a significant difference with a non-parametric test?'

'Correct – so it's worth finding out if it is possible to use a parametric test.'

If I was deciding whether to play a record on my mono player or my stereo I would go through a series of decisions (Figure 1.4).

Depending on the answer to each question I would decide which player to use:

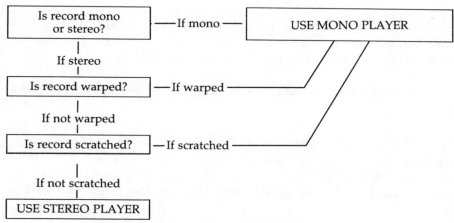

Fig 1.4: Decision tree for mono/stereo record player

Copy Figure 1.5 and use the information in the text to build a decision tree for deciding whether to use a parametric or non-parametric test.

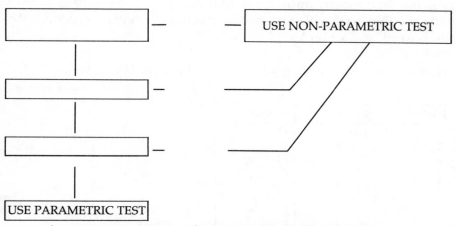

Fig 1.5: Decision tree for parametric/non-parametric test

Jo recommended that we used the **sign test** as it was the simplest test and could be used on almost any set of data. She explained that the sign test was a rough and ready test that could be used as an indication of whether or not there was a significant difference. The other tests in the book were more sophisticated and could only be used with results that had certain patterns and characteristics.

'So if this test says that there is less than 1 in 20 chance that the difference could have happened by chance ... I've won,' I said excitedly.

'Well if you want to be so competitive about it you could see it that way, but a more scientific way of looking at it is that the test will tell us whether or not we can reject the null hypothesis.'

'You make it sound as though you've got no personal interest in the results!'

'It's called being objective about it rather than subjective – which is what you're being,' she said. 'Anyway as this is only a small pilot study and not a full-blown study with lots of subjects, I think we should accept a lower significance level of less than one in ten $(p < 0.1)$.'

'That's alright by me ... You're giving me a better chance of being right.'

'True, but we'll have less confidence in the results. Anyway the first thing it says we have to do to the results is put them into pairs, and I presume that means putting the first trial with the cheap shampoo with the first trial with the second shampoo, and the second with the second, and so on.'

'That's easy,' I said and quickly drew up a table (Table 1.4).

Trial	Cheap	Expensive
1	11	13
2	7	11
3	15	12
4	9	10
5	10	11
6	8	9
7	9	14
8	9	11
9	7	11
10	10	12

Table 1.4

'Then draw another column and give each pair of scores a + sign if the left-hand score is bigger, or a − sign if the right-hand score is bigger.' (Table 1.5)

Trial	Cheap	Expensive	Sign
1	11	13	+
2	7	11	+
3	15	12	−
4	9	10	+
5	10	11	+
6	8	9	+
7	9	14	+
8	9	11	+
9	7	11	+
10	10	12	+

Table 1.5

'Count up the total number of signs; which is ten. So T = 10. Then count up the least frequent sign, which is −. As it occurs once, L = 1.'

'Then what?' I asked.
'That's it,' she said.
'Well, have I won?' I said.
'We have to look the result up in a table,' said Jo.

The table looked like Table 1.6:

L =	0	1	2	3	4	5	6
T = 5	0.062	0.376	1				
6	0.032	0.218	0.688	1			
7	0.016	0.124	0.454	1			
8	0.008	0.070	0.290	0.726	1		
9	0.004	0.040	0.180	0.508	1		
10	0.002	0.022	0.110	0.344	0.754	1	
11	0.000	0.012	0.066	0.226	0.582	1	
12	0.000	0.006	0.038	0.146	0.388	0.774	1

The probability of finding a number of less frequent signs (L) out of a total number of signs (T) for a two-tailed test. Adapted from Robson, C *Experimental Design and Statistics*, Penguin, 1964.

Table 1.6

In our experiment we had values of:

L = 1
T = 10

If the table is read off using these values, it shows a probability of:

p = 0.022

'So the probability level of $p = 0.022$ is less than the significance level of $p = 0.1$,' I said gleefully.

'Yes, and it's even lower than the "normal" significance level of $p = 0.05$.'

Questions

1 Copy Table 1.7 and apply the sign test.

Trial	Set A	Set B	Sign
1	10	9	
2	11	8	
3	10	11	
4	11	10	
5	9	10	
6	10	9	
7	11	8	
8	12	10	
9	10	9	

T =
L =
Table value: p =

In this example with a significance level of $p < 0.05$ we would:
(Accept? Reject?) the null hypothesis

Table 1.7

2 Try constructing a table and applying the sign test to the following sets of data, using a significance level of $p < 0.01$, and the table of values on the previous page.

Set C: 8, 10, 11, 10, 11, 10, 8, 11, 12, 9, 10, 9.

Set D: 9, 9, 12, 12, 12, 13, 10, 12, 13, 10, 11, 12.

3 In the above examples when the null hypothesis has been rejected, what are the confidence levels for accepting the experimental hypothesis?

Jo wrote down our results formally:

The sign test found a significant difference ($p < 0.1$, T = 10, L = 1, two-tailed) therefore we are able to reject the null hypothesis and accept the experimental hypothesis.

'What does it mean when it says two-tailed test?'

'Well, any test can be either one- or two-tailed. It makes no difference to how you work it out, but it makes a difference to the table you use to interpret the results.'

'How do you know which one to use?'

'It depends on your hypothesis. If your hypothesis predicts the direction of the experimental effect, eg changes in the independent variable will increase the values of the dependent variable, or changes in the independent variable will decrease the values of dependent variable, then you use the table for the one-tailed version of the test. But our hypothesis needed a two-tailed test because we said that the independent variable will affect the dependent variable.'

Questions

Which of the following are one-tailed hypotheses:

- There will be a difference in a teacher's level of anxiety depending on the amount of chalk in the room.
- Increased alcohol will decrease Space Invader performance.
- Space Invader performance will be affected by an increased amount of alcohol.
- The amount of rubbish dropped on the canteen floor will be less when red dustbins are used than when black dustbins are used.

'But I could have told you that the expensive shampoo would need more combings,' I remarked.

'Yes,' Jo replied, 'but you only use a one-tailed hypothesis if there is past research that suggests your results will go in a particular direction, or if your experiment is testing a theory that predicts the direction. And before you say it, I didn't think your original study was enough evidence to make it a one-tailed hypothesis.'

'I was actually going to ask if it would have made any difference?'

'No, it wouldn't have in this case, but one-tailed tests do give significant results for smaller differences than two-tailed tests.'

'So if we didn't get a significant difference we could have changed our hypothesis to a one-tailed one and got a significant result?'

'Well it would be very tempting, but I'm afraid it isn't allowed. The hypothesis should be set before you carry out the experiment, and the type of test follows the type of hypothesis. One drawback of using a one-tailed hypothesis is that if the results show a difference

31

that is in the opposite direction to the prediction, this must be counted as no difference at all.'

Smugly happy that the results had come out in support of my hypothesis, I composed a letter to the paper telling them of our findings.

Dear Sirs,

My colleague and I have discovered a major fraud that is being carried out by the chemical companies that manufacture shampoos. We have conducted an experiment that proves that buying expensive shampoos is a complete waste of money, because they contain a tangling agent that means you have to use an untangling agent which they call a conditioner.

In our study we compared the number of combings needed to get my hair tangle free, after washing with an expensive and a cheap shampoo. We took many precautions to ensure that both shampoos were given the same chance, and the results proved that the cheap shampoo produced less tangling.

This proves that the shampoo manufacturers are conning the public into wasting more money than is necessary by forcing them to buy a conditioner with an already expensive shampoo.

I showed the letter to Jo, and she collapsed into fits of giggles. 'You were cut out to be a journalist rather than a scientist,' she said. 'You've made a sensational claim on the basis on very flimsy evidence.'

'But you saw the results of the statistical test,' I protested.

'Yes, but that doesn't mean that we can make fantastic generalisations like you have.'

She wrote a section of a scientific report:

Discussion of results

The results were generally supportive of the hypothesis. Between 1.9 and 2 more combings were needed to get the subject's hair tangle free when the expensive shampoo was used. One result went against the general trend with the highest number of combings needed for a trial of the cheap shampoo.

The results were significant at a much higher level than we would have been prepared to accept for a pilot study, and this gives a firm suggestion that there could be a factor in this expensive shampoo that tangles people's hair.

Before any definite conclusions are made there is need for further research as this study obviously has its limitations. Only one subject was used – a regular user of cheap shampoo – and it is a possibility that their hair had adapted to this type of cleanser. Also the reliability of the measure used must be questioned as there are difficulties in keeping the same pressure on a comb manually.

Questions

1 Compare Jo's report with my letter. What have I claimed in my letter that cannot be definitely supported by the experiment?

2 Jo mentioned in her report that there would be difficulty in keeping the same pressure with a comb by hand. Because of this, the measure used might not be consistent or **reliable**. As well as the consistency or reliability of measures that we take in experiments, we have to be concerned with the **validity** of the measures, ie whether they actually measure what we say they are measuring. Our measure of combing does not directly measure whether a chemical is specially put in to tangle the hair (although this might be the case), it only measures how tangled the hair is.

Which of the following do you think are valid measures of a person's arithmetical ability? For each example explain why.

a Their results in an English exam
b How neatly they write their numbers
c The number of times they use a calculator in a maths exam
d The speed with which they can solve arithmetical problems

3 Copy the paragraph below and complete it by the inserting the words reliable, reliability, valid and validity in the appropriate space.

The _____ of a measure refers to whether it can be taken consistently. If I measure the size of a person's head using a tape measure, and each time I measure this person's head I get the same result, this means that my measure is _____. I would be a fool to say that this was a _____ measure of how intelligent the person is, as intelligence is not related to the size of a person's head. The _____ of a measure refers to whether it measures what the experimenter says it does.

2 Experimental designs

In any experiment the researcher wishes to know whether the independent variable affects the dependent variable. The dependent variable is usually a 'performance' measure, eg reaction time, number of words recalled, score on a test.

The independent variable sets the conditions the dependent variable is measured under. In simple experiments, the researcher measures performance on the dependent variable at two levels (or values) of the independent variable. These levels are called the **conditions** of the experiment.

In two of the designs (the independent groups design and the matched groups design), the subjects are separated into two groups. Each group is then treated in a different way, ie each group's performance or the dependent variable is measured under a different condition.

The independent groups design

This is the simplest and roughest design. Figure 2.1 shows the procedure:

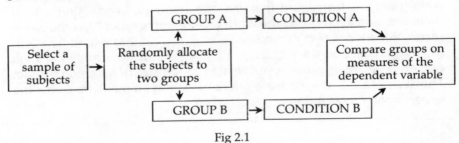

Fig 2.1

Questions

1 An experiment was designed using the independent groups design to test the following hypothesis:

The amount of alcohol drunk will affect performance on a Space Invader machine.

The researchers compared the effects of drinking no alcohol with drinking three pints of beer.

a What is the independent variable?
b What is the dependent variable?
c What are the levels of the independent variable (or what are the conditions of the experiment)?
d It is well known that alcohol impairs motor performance. In this experiment Space Invader scores are being used as a measure of motor performance. If the results showed that there was no difference between the two groups' performance how might these results be explained?

A problem with the independent groups design

The independent groups design provides data that contains many impurities. The biggest problem is that if there is a difference between the two groups in their performance on the dependent variable this could be caused by two things:

1 An experimental effect, ie the independent variable did affect the dependent variable.

2 Inter-subject variability. This is the technical term for the fact that individuals differ in their ability on any particular measure. In the alcohol and space invaders example, there's a chance that all of one group could be Space Invader experts. Variability between subjects could be the cause of either difference, or lack of difference, between the groups. Intersubject variability can thus confound the results of an independent groups design.

The matched groups design

This is a more sensitive design but it can be fiddly. Figure 2.2 shows the procedure:

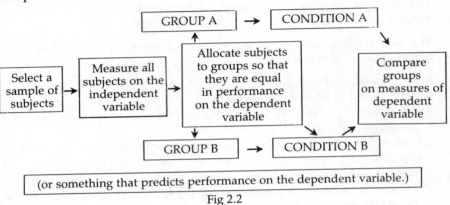

Fig 2.2

Example

Suppose we wanted to test the hypothesis about alcohol and space invader performance. Having selected our sample we could then measure all subjects on a Space Invader machine:

subject 1 150
subject 2 3000
subject 3 500
subject 4 150
subject 5 3000
subject 6 4500
etc

subjects 1 and 4 make a matched pair, and so do subjects 2 and 5, therefore we can put one of each pair into each group:

GROUP A: SUBJECTS 1 AND 2
GROUP B: SUBJECTS 4 AND 5

Notice that some subjects (ie 3 and 6) will not be used in the experiment because there is not another subject available as an exact match. (In practice, subjects rarely get exactly the same scores so very similar scores are used to match subjects.)

Alternatively the matching might be carried out on another computer game that predicts performance on the Space Invader machine. If we know from previous studies that all subjects who get high scores on a Galacticans game also get high scores on Space Invaders, and similarly those who get low scores on Galacticans get low scores on Space Invaders, we could match the groups on performance on Galacticans. This would have the advantage that the subjects did not get any practice on the Space Invaders game before they were measured under the conditions of the experiment.

36

Questions

1 Copy the following sentence and fill in the gaps:

The matched groups design is a more sensitive design than the independent groups design because it avoids _____-_____ ____ _____?

2 Suppose there is another computer game called Galacticans, and it is found that a person's scores on Galacticans predicts their performance on a Space Invader machine. Copy the axes below (Figure 2.3) and draw a line to represent this relationship:

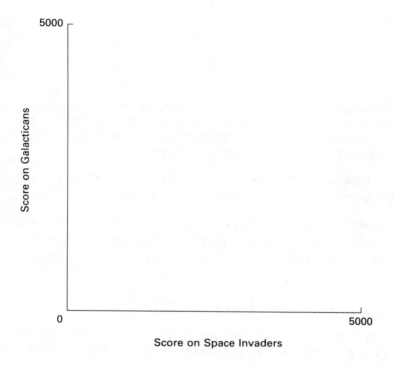

Fig 2.3

3 Can you think of any reason why researchers sometimes prefer to match subjects on a measure that predicts performance on the dependent variable, rather than matching them on the dependent variable itself?

4 Table 2.1 below shows scores taken from a sample of subjects. The scores represent speed of reading a 100 word paragraph. Create two matched groups from the data.

Subject number	Reading speed in seconds
1	18
2	15
3	23
4	18
5	21
6	27
7	15
8	24
9	24
10	32
11	16
12	23
13	31
14	21

Table 2.1

5 By taking the subject numbers and putting them into a hat and pulling them out at random, it would be possible to randomly assign the subjects to groups as in an independent groups design. Try doing this and find the difference between the two groups.

The independent groups design is less sensitive because the results it provides can be confounded by inter-subject variability.

The matched groups design is more sensitive as it controls for inter-subject variability by matching subjects on the dependent variable prior to testing them under the conditions of the experiment.

The repeated measures design

The repeated measures design is the most sensitive design. It completely removes the possibility of inter-subject variability by using each subject in both conditions of the experiment.

Figure 2.4 shows the procedure for the repeated measures design:

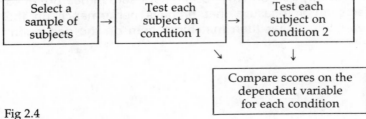

Fig 2.4

Example

Suppose we wanted to test whether alcohol affects performance on a Space Invader machine (Figure 2.5).

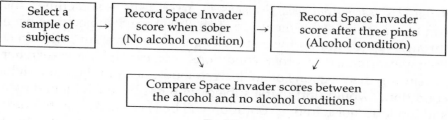

Fig 2.5

Questions

1 Draw and fill in a diagram to represent a repeated measures design testing the hypothesis that:

The level of light in a room will affect the time taken to sort a pack of cards into four suits.

2 In the alcohol and Space Invader example why did the experimenter choose to have the no alcohol condition before the alcohol condition?

Order effects

In a repeated measures design the same subjects are measured on the dependent variable under two conditions. This can cause problems because:

1 *Subjects learn from experience* – because of this their performance on a task may improve simply because they have had practice. For example, if the repeated measures design was used to test whether different lighting conditions affected performance on a card-sorting task, the subjects might have faster sorting times in the second lighting condition simply because they have had more practice at the card-sorting task. This is called a **practice effect**.

2 *Subjects get tired* – in very long experiments where the subject is expected to do a lot of work their performance towards the end of the experiment may get worse simply because they are getting tired. This is often called a **fatigue effect**.

3 *Subjects get bored* – again, in long experiments in which the subject is expected to do a lot of work, the subject's performance may get

progressively worse not because of the conditions of the experiment but simply because they become bored. Not surprisingly, this is called a boredom effect.

4 *Subjects learn from what happens in experiments* – sometimes the conditions of an experiment are such that once a subject has been through one condition their knowledge of the procedure will affect their performance in other conditions. For example, a researcher measuring the reactions of subjects to loud noises in dark and light conditions, would find that a subject who has been frightened by a sudden loud noise in one condition will be less shocked in the next condition because they will be expecting the possibility of a loud noise. This is called a **knowledge effect**.

These problems with the repeated measures design come under the collective heading of **order effects**. There are other order effects but the most common ones are the practice, fatigue, boredom, and knowledge effects mentioned above.

Questions

1 There are three types of experimental design, each with its own advantages and disadvantages. Draw a table like the one below and put the listed statements in the appropriate place. (Each statement can be used more than once.)

Results can be confounded by inter-subject variability
Results can be confounded by order effects
Results cannot be confounded by order effects
Is wasteful because some subjects have to be discarded
Is economical because it only uses subjects in more than one condition
Is uneconomical because it only uses each subject once
Results cannot be confounded by inter-subject variability

Type of design	Advantages	Disadvantages

Counterbalancing and randomisation – ways of reducing order effects

If the order effects are expected to be large or if there is a knowledge effect: do not use the repeated measures design.

If the practice effect is expected to be large and the aim of the experiment is to measure skilled performance under different conditions: give the subjects a practice session before they are measured under the conditions of the experiment.

If the order effects are expected to be small: use *counterbalancing* or *randomisation*.

Counterbalancing

There are two types of counterbalancing:

1 *Counterbalancing across subjects* – in this form of counterbalancing half the subjects carry out the conditions in one order and half the subjects carry out the conditions in the reverse order. So, for example, if there are two conditions, condition A and condition B:

Half the subjects are measured under condition A, then condition B;
Half the subjects are measured under condition B, then condition A.

Therefore half the subjects have the benefit of practice in condition B and half the benefit of practice in condition A. This means that when the scores of all the subjects are looked at together the effects of practice will be balanced out.

2 *Counterbalancing within subjects* – in this form of counterbalancing each subject is measured twice under each condition. So, for example, each subject is measured under condition A, then B, then B, and then A. (It is easy to see why this is sometimes called the ABBA design.)

This solution relies on the assumption that there are competing order effects that work in a symmetrical way. In the first measurement of condition A the subject will not have had any practice, but will not be fatigued or bored. By the last measurement of condition A they will be fatigued and bored but will have had the most practice.

41

Randomisation

Randomisation works on the principle that if the ordering of conditions is assigned randomly the chances are that order effects will cancel themselves out. Unlike counterbalancing it does not assume that the order effects are symmetrical or consistent across subjects. In randomisation the order in which each subject completes conditions is determined by chance, eg the result of a toss of a coin. For example, if there are two conditions, A and B, with each subject measured once in each condition:

If the coin lands heads up: subject does condition A, then condition B. If the coin lands tails up: subject does condition B, then condition A.

Similarly, if the subject is to be measured more than once under each condition the ordering of conditions can be achieved by tossing a coin.

Questions

	X			Y			Z	
Subject number	Order of conditions		Subject number	Order of conditions		Subject number	Order of conditions	
1	AB		1	BA		1	AB	
2	BA		2	AB		2	BA	
3	AB		3	BA		3	BA	
4	BA		4	AB		4	BA	
5	AB		5	BA		5	BA	
6	BA		6	AB		6	AB	
7	AB		7	AB		7	AB	
8	BA		8	AB		8	AB	

Table 2.2

1 Which of the examples in Table 2.2: X, Y or Z, is not counterbalanced?

2 Are the others counterbalanced within or across subjects?

3 When each subject is being measured twice in both conditions it is possible to counterbalance both within and across subjects. Copy and complete Table 2.3 so that it is counterbalanced both ways:

Subject number	Order of conditions
1	ABBA
2	
3	
4	
5	
6	
7	
8	

Table 2.3

4 Explain what is wrong with the following statements:

a Counterbalancing can balance out all order effects.
b Counterbalancing gets rid of practice effects.

3 Advantages and disadvantages of the mean, median and mode

Each measure of central tendency or average is worked out in a different way. This means that on many occasions you will get different answers for the mean, median and mode. The question then arises: which one is the most appropriate or representative? This question can only be answered if you know the advantages and disadvantages of each.

For each average we must ask the following questions:

1 Does the average get affected by extreme scores?

2 Is the average always an actual score within the set of scores?

3 Does the average use all of the scores in its calculation?

4 Does the average use all of the values of the scores in its calculation?

Example: The arithmetic mean

The arithmetic mean is affected by extreme scores: eg the set of scores: 5, 5, 5, 5, 180 has a mean of 40. The mean is made larger by the one extreme score of 180. This is a disadvantage as one extreme score can greatly affect the value of the mean.

It is also clear from the above example that the mean is not always an actual score within the set of scores. This is a disadvantage especially when we are dealing with scores that cannot be meaningfully divided into fractions, eg the mean number of children in a family is 2.4. What is meant by 0.4 of a child?

However, in calculating the mean we do use all of the scores and all the value of the scores. Therefore it has the advantage of using all the information available.

44

Questions

1 Copy and complete Table 3.1 to allow a comparison of the advantages and disadvantages of the mean, median and mode.

	Advantages	Disadvantages
Mean	1 Uses all the scores 2 Uses all the values of the scores	1 Is affected by extreme scores 2 Is not always an actual score
Median		
Mode		

Table 3.1

2 Discrete measures can only have particular values; eg the measure of the number of children in a family is discrete, as it is not meaningful to talk about subdivisions of a child.

Continuous measures can have any value; eg the measure: the height of women is a continuous variable as you can meaningfully have subdivisions of inches or centimetres.

Which of the following are continuous measures, and which discrete:

a Shoe size
b Temperature in centigrade
c Reaction time
d Weekly income in pounds and pence

3 A country has a few people with very fast reading speeds and the large majority of people with slow reading speeds. If you wanted to find the average reading speed of people in that country, which average would be the most representative? Which would be the least representative?

Scales of measurement . . . or different ways of using numbers

Hardly numbers – more like names

The simplest way in which numbers are used is as names. Used as names they have no size, so they cannot be added, subtracted, multiplied or divided. For example, if there are three people: Clive, Indira, and Joel and we assign each one a number:

Clive = 1
Indira = 2
Joel = 3

we cannot add 1 and 2 to make 3, otherwise we would be saying that Clive + Indira = Joel which doesn't make much sense. When numbers are used as names our data is called **nominal data**.

The most common form of nominal data used in psychology is when a researcher has counted the number of times an event occurs. This is called **frequency data**. For example, if we wanted to know the number of times a particular name is used we would count the frequency of use. So if in a thousand births:

Clive is used four times its frequency is 4
Indira is used once its frequency is 1
Joel is used five times its frequency is 5

When numbers are used instead of names, or when the frequency of an event or category is counted, this provides **nominal** data.

Just numbers . . . at least they have size

Most often when we use numbers we do so because numbers allow us to put things in size order.
When psychologists measure people's abilities by using question-

46

naire tests they are able to say that one person achieves a higher or lower score than another person. For example, if on an IQ test

Clive scores 90
Indira scores 120
Joel scores 100

we can say that Indira's IQ score is greater than Joel's, which is greater than Clive's.

We might be tempted to say that there is twice as much difference between Indira and Joel as there is between Joel and Clive, but unfortunately questionnaires are not equal interval scales. That is, when we use questionnaires we are not sure of the distance between adjacent points on the scale. For example the difference (interval) between a score of 99 and a score of 100 may not be the same as the difference between a score of 100 and a score of 101.

Measuring devices such as questionnaires allow us to put scores into size order, but do not allow us to know the exact size of the difference between two scores.

Data that can be put into size order where the difference in size is either unmeasureable or not known is called **ordinal data**.

More like normal . . . the interval scale

When we measure something in feet and inches, or centimetres and metres, or minutes and seconds, we know that each unit of measurement is equal in size. That is, each centimetre equals every other centimetre.

In this form of measurement we know that we can place scores into size order and that the size of the difference between any two scores is equal.

When numbers are used in this way the data is called **interval data**.

The Ratio Scale

A ratio scale of measurement is simply an interval scale in which it is impossible to get a negative value ie there is an absolute zero point. For example, it is impossible to have a negative reaction time.

Questions

To establish whether a dependent variable provides nominal, ordinal, interval or ratio data it is possible to ask a number of questions and then work out what type of data it is. Figure 4.1 includes the questions that have to be asked – but the types of data are not filled in. Copy the diagram and complete it.

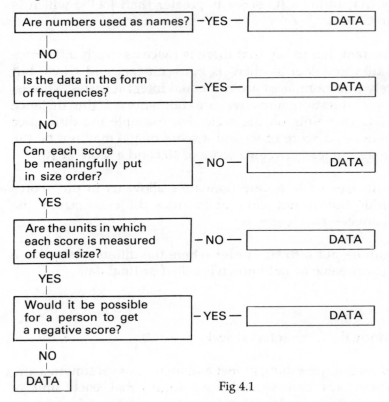

Fig 4.1

Now use the table and the text to decide what kind of data the following examples are:

a A person's height
b Number of letters that a person can hold in short-term memory
c Scores from an attitude questionnaire
d Numbers on football jerseys
e Position in a class exam – eg 1st, 2nd . . .
f Percentage mark in exam

5 Variance and standard deviation

Roughly speaking, variance is a measure of how spread out a set of scores is. You have already been introduced to one measure of spread: range. So why do we need another one? The answer lies in the fact that variance is a more sophisticated measure than range.

To put it more exactly: the variance is a statistic that represents the average distance of each score from the mean of the set.

This means that the variance is more informative than the range, because when the range is worked out only the largest and smallest scores are used. The range, therefore, ignores the values of the large majority of scores and can describe two very different sets of scores as though they are the same. As the variance uses the values of *all* of the scores, it can describe the spread of the scores in more detail.

Questions

1 Compare these two sets of scores by working out the mean scores and the range for each set.

Set A: 2, 3, 4, 5, 6 4
Set B: 2, 4, 4, 4, 6 4

As you can see these descriptive statistics do not help to distinguish between these two groups.

2 Now try plotting Set B on a frequency distribution like the one in Figure 5.1.

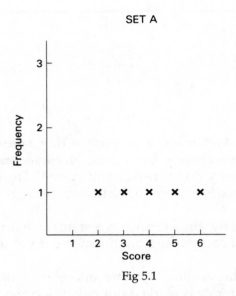

Fig 5.1

a In which set are the scores on average closer to the mean? (Which is on average the 'thinner' distribution?)

b Combine your answer to the last question with the definition of the variance above. Which set has the smaller variance?

How to work out the variance and the standard deviation

To compute variance:

1 Find the mean

2 Find the difference between each score and the mean

3 Multiply each difference by itself (squaring)

4 Add up all the squared differences

5 Divide the total by the number of scores minus one

It can be helpful to use a table like Table 5.1.

A	B	C	D
Score	Mean score	Difference between score and mean	Difference squared
2	4	−2	4
3		−1	1
4		0	0
5		+1	1
6		+2	4
TOTAL = 20			TOTAL = 10

Number of scores = 5; Number of scores minus one = 4

Table 5.1

I put all the scores in column A and added them all up. By dividing this total by the number of scores, I obtained the mean, which I put in column B. I then subtracted column B from column A (eg $2 - 4 = -2$) and entered the result in column C. Column D is column C squared, eg $-2 \times -2 = 4$. Column D is then totalled.

Once all this has been worked out, the variance can be found by dividing the total of column D by the number of scores minus one. Variance = $10 \div 4 = 2.5$.

The standard deviation

The standard deviation is simply the square root of the variance. So for Set A, the square root of 2.5 = 1.58.

You will see later that the standard deviation has uses when dividing up the normal distribution.

Questions

1 Draw a table like Table 5.1 and work out the variance for Set B (on page 49).

2 What is the standard deviation for Set B?

Mathematical symbols for variance and standard deviation

You will often come across the variance and the standard deviation written in mathematical formulae. The symbols are as follows:
    Σ means the total of
    $\bar{x}$ means the arithmetic mean

51

x means the scores

( ) means work this bit out first before you try to do the things outside the brackets

$(\ )^2$ means the square of what's inside the bracket

$\sqrt{\ }$ means the square root of

n means the number of scores

Example

In words the formula for the arithmetic mean is:

$$\text{the mean} = \frac{\text{the total of the scores}}{\text{the number of the scores}}$$

so: Σ means the total of

x means the score

n means the number of scores

Therefore the formula is: $\bar{x} = \dfrac{\Sigma x}{n}$

In words the formula for the variance is:

$$\text{the variance} = \frac{\text{the total of (the difference between the mean and each score) squared}}{\text{the number of scores minus one}}$$

Questions

1 Use the table of symbols to write the mathematical formulae for the variance.

2 Now do the same for the standard deviation.

come back to this

6 Normal distribution

The normal distribution is the name given to a particular pattern of scores. When plotted on a frequency distribution graph this pattern of scores produces the symmetrical bell shape shown in Figure 6.1.

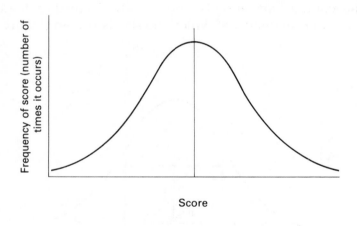

Fig 6.1

It is of use to statisticians and many others because its mathematical properties are known and are used in certain types of tests called parametric tests.

Properties of the normal distribution

Because it is symmetrical the three averages (mean, median and mode) are exactly the same. This means that the average score divides the distribution into exactly equal halves (Figure 6.2).

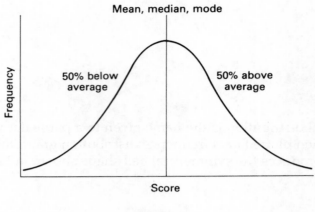

Fig 6.2

When the standard deviation is worked out, this further divides the distribution into segments of which the size is shown (Figure 6.3).

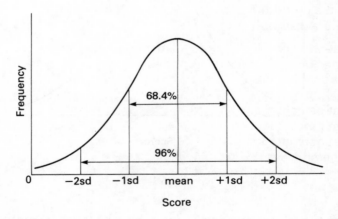

Fig 6.3

Psychologists have found that by adjusting IQ tests they can make the population of IQ scores fit the normal distribution. The overall pattern looks roughly like that shown in Figure 6.4.

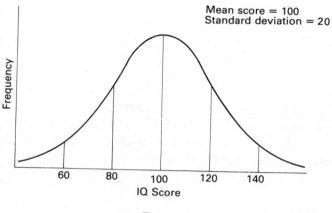

Fig 6.4

Questions

Using the properties of the normal distribution and remembering that the whole distribution will equal 100%, work out the following:

a What percentage of people have an IQ above 100?
b If a person were picked at random from the population, what would be the probability of them having an IQ of over 100?
c What percentage of people have an IQ between 100 and 120?
d What percentage have an IQ above 140?
e What percentage have an IQ above 60?
f What percentage have IQs between 60 and 80?
g If a person were picked at random from the population, what is the probability that they would have an IQ of less than 60?
h If a sample of ten people were picked at random from the population, which is the most probable mean IQ of the sample: 80, 100, 120?
i Can you explain why your answer to h is the most likely mean IQ score of the sample?

MD

55

7 Errors and design

When designing an experiment we are trying to isolate the effects of the independent variable on the dependent variable, ie the **experimental effect**. This effect can be confounded by two types of error: constant errors and random errors.

Constant errors

These are errors that affect the scores in one condition of an experiment in the same way, causing all of these scores to be either increased or decreased. For example, if two lists of words are used in a memory experiment and list A is easier to learn than list B, subjects may get a higher recall score with list A than list B, regardless of the conditions. Or, if one group of subjects is given longer to do a test than another group they may get higher scores because they have more time.

The constant errors above are the result of design faults. They are caused by the experimenter not controlling potential independent variables.

When using the independent groups design a constant error can occur if the performance of one group is better than the other group, regardless of the effect of the independent variable. This is less likely to occur if large groups are used and the subjects are randomly allocated to conditions.

When using the repeated measures design order effects can introduce constant errors. These can be minimised by using counterbalancing or randomisation which spreads the effects of the errors across conditions.

Constant errors can obscure an experimental effect and cause the experimenter to conclude that there was no effect when there was, or they can cause a difference in results when there wasn't an experimental effect.

Constant errors can be eliminated (or minimised) by carefully designing experiments to control for possible sources of constant error.

Random errors

These are more troublesome because they cannot be eliminated – they can only be kept to a minimum. Random errors occur due to:

1 Intra-subject variability. Individuals vary in their performance on a task over time, ie individuals are not consistent in their performance.

2 Small potential independent variables that cannot be identified or controlled for. These include variations in environmental factors, eg lighting or noise, and personal factors, eg personality and experience.

Random errors, experimental designs and statistical tests

The problem of random errors means that we need statistical tests to process the data of our experiments. Random errors are the cause of what might be called fluke results. In well-designed experiments any difference between the results of different conditions will be caused by: 1) the effect of the independent variable on the dependent variable, ie the experimental effect; and/or 2) the effect of random errors.

The results from an independent groups design are more likely to be affected by random error than those from a matched subject or repeated measures design. This is because groups can still differ because of the effects of inter-subject variability, even when large groups are used and subjects are randomly allocated to groups. Tests that process the results from independent group designs must therefore allow for larger chance differences than the tests that process the results of matched subject or repeated measures designs.

Questions

1 Copy out the paragraph below, including the correct word from each pair of alternatives in the gaps.

When designing an experiment we try to keep everything constant in each condition to avoid the effects of RANDOM/CONSTANT errors. Even if we control everything that we can think of, there is still the possibility that there are small uncontrollable variables that are RANDOM/CONSTANT errors. If we use the matched subjects or the repeated measures design we can control for INTRA-/INTER-subject variability, but we can never control for INTER-/INTRA-subject availability. In the repeated measures design there is the possibility that order effects will introduce CONSTANT/RANDOM errors, but these can be minimised through _____ or _____. The results of an independent groups design are likely to differ LESS/MORE than the results of matched subject or repeated measures designs, because of RANDOM/CONSTANT errors.

2 Using the information given in the text and below, copy the table, putting the tests in their proper places to complete the table.

Parametric tests assume that data is interval.

Non-parametric tests assume that data is at least ordinal.

	Parametric test	Non-parametric tests
Independent groups design	_____test	_____test
Matched subjects *or* Repeated measures design	_____test	_____test or _____test

Independent t-test: Assumes data is interval and allows for inter-subject variability

Wilcoxon test: Assumes data can be put into size order and does not allow for inter-subject variability

Correlated t-test: Assumes data is interval and does not allow for inter-subject variability

Sign test: Assumes data is ordinal, and does not allow for inter-subject variability

Mann-Whitney U-test: Assumes data is ordinal and allows for inter-subject variability.

58

8 Correlation

Have you ever noticed that the more people there are in a room the warmer the room seems to be? If you have, one way of stating this is to say that you have noticed a relationship between the number of people in the room and the temperature. You have combined observations that you have made and decided that there is a relationship between two variables:

Variable 1: number of people in the room
Variable 2: the temperature

In statistics, relationships between two variables are plotted on a graph called a scattergram. Figure 8.1 shows three scattergrams showing different types of relationship, and below them are three descriptions of relationships in words. Can you match up the graphs with the descriptions?

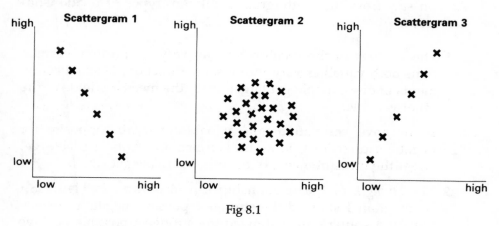

Fig 8.1

Positive correlation: High scores on one variable tend to go together with high scores on the other variable.

Negative correlation: High scores on one variable tend to go together with low scores on the other variable, eg large class sizes tend to mean small amounts of individual attention for students from teachers; a small class size tends to mean larger amounts of individual attention.

Zero correlation: There is no relationship between the scores on one variable and the scores on the other variable.

Questions

1 What type of correlation is shown in: **a** Scattergram 1, **b** Scattergram 2, and **c** Scattergram 3?

2 Copy and complete the following sentences, including the correct alternative.

When there is a positive correlation, as measurements of one variable increase the measurements of the other variable tend to DECREASE/INCREASE.

When there is a negative correlation, as measurements of one variable increase the measurements of the other variable tend to INCREASE/DECREASE.

When there is no relationship between the measurements of two variables the variables show a POSITIVE CORRELATION/ZERO CORRELATION/NEGATIVE CORRELATION.

As you saw from the scattergrams, different types of relationship can occur:

1 The *direction* of the relationship can vary. In positive correlations both variables vary in the same direction, ie as measurements of one variable get larger so do the measurements of the other variable.

In negative correlations the variables vary in opposite (or negative) directions, ie as measurements of one variable get larger the measurements of the other variable get smaller.

2 The *strength* of the relationship can also vary. In Figure 8.1 scattergram 1 showed the strongest possible negative correlation, and scattergram 3 showed the strongest possible positive correlation. They were what is called a 'perfect negative correlation' and a 'perfect positive correlation'. Scattergram 2) showed the weakest possible correlation, ie no relationship at all.

The strength and the direction of a correlation can be summarised by a statistic known as a **correlation coefficient**. Correlation coefficients are numbers that vary in size between −1 and +1. Figure 8.2 shows examples of scattergrams showing a range of relationships with their correlation coefficients.

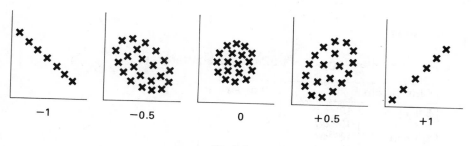

Fig 8.2

NB. The sign (+ or −) indicates the direction of the relationship (positive or negative) and the size of the number indicates the strength of the relationship (0 is the weakest, 1 is the strongest).

How to interpret correlations

The most common mistake made when a correlation is found is to automatically assume that one variable causes the other to vary. A causal relationship is only one of three possible explanations for a correlation. The three possible explanations are:

1 A causal relationship

2 Both variables are affected by a third variable

3 The correlation occurs by chance (often called a spurious correlation)

Example

A perfect positive correlation is found between the number of storks in Stockholm and the number of babies born.

Causal explanation: The increase in storks causes an increase in babies (I think this unlikely, from my limited knowledge of biology!).

Third variable explanation: Variations in the weather cause the number of storks to vary. As it gets colder they fly away, as it gets

61

they return. Babies are planned for the spring to give them a better chance of survival.

Or it could just be a *chance correlation*.

Questions

1 Plot the following set of points on a scattergram:

Girls' height		Shoe size
5 ft 11 in	180 cm	8
5 ft 0 in	152 cm	3
5 ft 6 in	167 cm	5
5 ft 1 in	155 cm	3
5 ft 5 in	165 cm	6
5 ft 9 in	175 cm	7
5 ft 1 in	155 cm	4
5 ft 3 in	160 cm	4
5 ft 0 in	152 cm	4

a Is the correlation positive or negative?
b Is the correlation fairly strong or weak?

2 Which of the three possible explanations for a correlation do you think is most likely in the examples below? In each case state the most likely explanation, and give your reasons why you think it is the most likely.

a A negative correlation between the distance from earth of Haley's Comet and the price of petrol.
b A positive correlation between the size of a person's house and the size of their car.
c A negative correlation between memory effectiveness and the amount of revision needed to pass exams.

9 Samples and populations

How representative is your class of the population of Great Britain?

In psychology, studies are carried out on samples of subjects, and it is hoped that the results can then be generalised to a wider population. By *generalise* we mean that the results from the samples are taken to hold true for the population in general. This process of generalisation is only possible if the sample is 'representative' of the population, ie the sample has the same characteristics as the overall population.

Questions

1 Copy and fill in Table 9.1 and compare some characteristics of your group with the overall percentages.

Characteristic	Population percentage	Number in group with characteristic	% of group	Higher/ lower/ same
Right-handed	88–90			
White Caucasian	95			
First born children	41			
Fourth or later born	9			
Smoking (16–19 yr olds)	30			
Defects in colour vision*	male 8 female 0.5			
5 or more GCE or GCSE A–C grades including CSE 1	male 10 female 12			

Table 9.1

* You can investigate this either by self-report, or by using colour plates that can be found in most introductory texts on Psychology under the topic of Perception.

2 You probably found that your class group was unrepresentative of the population of Great Britain on at least some of the measures. Can you think of any other ways in which your group is likely to be unrepresentative?

3 Can you think of a sub-section of the population of Great Britain of which your group is more likely to be representative?

A couple of definitions

Population: In psychology the word population means any definable group of people. So a few examples of populations are:

- all psychology students in Great Britain
- all three-year-olds in Basingstoke
- all people with ginger hair
- all schizophrenics in institutional care

Sample: A sample is a subsection selected from a population. When doing research in psychology it is usually to define the population that is to be studied, and then take a sample from this population.

Methods of sampling

As you have probably seen from the last exercise, it is not possible to take just any group of people and expect them to be representative of a population. Psychologists want to be able to generalise the results of their studies to a wider population, so they need standard methods of selecting samples. Some of the major methods are outlined below.

Random sampling

In this method each member of a population is given the same chance of being chosen for the sample. There are two main methods of doing this:

1 *The lottery method* – the name of each member of the population is put on a piece of paper. The pieces of paper are then put into a container (a hat, or a barrel). The sample is then selected by blindly picking out the required number of pieces of paper.

2 *Random number tables* – as before, each person in the population

is given a number but in this method the selection is determined by a series of random numbers that have been prepared by a method very similar to that described above.

Stratified random sampling

Sometimes when random sampling is used the sample may not be representative of the whole population that is being studied. This may be particularly true if the population has sub-groups that have different characteristics. These sub-groups of a population are called **strata**.

Example: Suppose the population we are sampling from is adults in Glasgow, and the strata we have identified in our population are the working class, middle class and upper class. We also know that these social classes are of different sizes, and we want our sample to be representative of this. The method of taking a sample of 100 people would be as follows (Table 9.2).

Overall population	Strata in population		
Adults in Glasgow	Working class	65% – Randomly select	65
	Middle class	30% – Randomly select	30
	Upper class	5% – Randomly select	5
		TOTAL SAMPLE	100

Table 9.2

Exercise in random sampling using random number tables

Table 9.3 shows the IQ scores of the population of a very small village consisting of 50 people. The people are not named but are called Person 1, Person 2, and so on through to Person 50 (this has been abbreviated to P1, P2, etc to P50).

Person	IQ score	Person	IQ score	Person	IQ score	Person	IQ score	Person	IQ score
P1	100	P11	90	P21	80	P31	100	P41	110
P2	120	P12	100	P22	100	P32	70	P42	80
P3	90	P13	110	P23	110	P33	120	P43	140
P4	140	P14	50	P24	90	P34	130	P44	90
P5	70	P15	110	P25	100	P35	70	P45	100
P6	110	P16	90	P26	130	P36	110	P46	120
P7	90	P17	100	P27	60	P37	100	P47	80
P8	90	P18	150	P28	120	P38	100	P48	100
P9	80	P19	120	P29	90	P39	60	P49	80
P10	110	P20	80	P30	110	P40	120	P50	130

Table 9.3

Table 9.4 is a small section of a random number table:

```
7 5 9 1 0 7 4 0 1 0 7 7 3 6 9 4 8 7 0 2 5 7 6 0 7 9 5 5 1 6 5 3
1 7 6 7 3 0 8 6 3 8 1 6 4 6 4 3 0 6 1 3 4 1 7 7 9 7 8 6 3 7 4 8
5 7 2 6 9 6 4 0 4 4 4 3 8 9 5 7 4 1 3 4 8 1 6 9 5 6 2 0 6 4 6 1
6 8 1 7 2 1 5 9 9 4 5 8 1 7 0 9 9 3 4 0 4 8 9 0 2 3 6 7 6 4 5 0
2 3 6 0 4 9 1 8 2 9 3 3 2 6 4 1 3 4 8 1 6 9 5 6 2 0 6 4 6 5 4 8
```

Table 9.4

Questions

1 Select a sample of 10 people using the table. You do this by closing your eyes and bringing your pencil down on part of the random number table. At the number where your pencil comes down start reading off the numbers in pairs to the right of that point. Once you have collected 10 pairs of numbers these are the numbers of the people that will be in your sample. Copy them into a table like the one below:

	P	P	P	P	P	P	P	P	P	P
SCORE										

2 When plotted on a histogram the population produces the following curve:

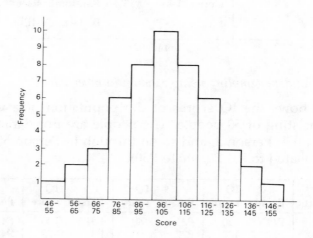

3 If you wanted to take a stratified random sample from your college, what might be appropriate strata?

Copy the diagram and add the data from your sample. How do the characteristics of the sample fit in with the population? Does it have the same mean, range, variance etc?

CROSSWORD ONE

ACROSS
3 A one line mini theory (10)
5 If you keep conditions constant you do this (7)
8 The variable that is measured (9)
10 In this type of blind experiment both the subject and the experimenter are unaware (6)
12 A type of difference not likely to happen by chance (11)
13 The most frequent score (4)
15 The person who manipulates 4 down (12)
17 These are types of 4 down that need controlling (9)
18 The aim of an experiment is to do this to the null hypothesis (7)

DOWN
1 Probability (6)
2 The middle score (6)
4 The variable that is manipulated (11)
6 The difference between the highest and lowest scores (5)
7 An average (7)
9 Chance or likelihood (11)
11 The results are analysed to find out if 4 down had one of these on 8 across (16)
14 Scores (4)
16 This type of hypothesis usually predicts no difference (4)

CROSSWORD TWO

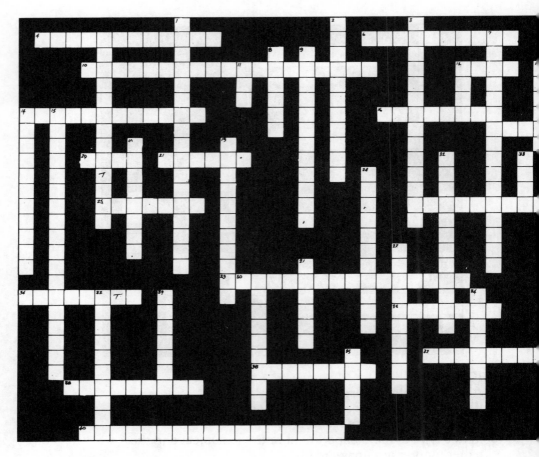

ACROSS

4 and 6 A one line mini theory tested by an experiment (12, 10)

10 The part that is manipulated or changed by the experimenter (11, 8)

12 The most frequent score (4)

14 Things that affect the results (but not in a constant way) (6)

16 The statistic that represents the average distance of each score from the mean (8)

17 This type of hypothesis usually predicts no difference (4)

20 Scores (4)

21 The middle score (6)

25 This type of data can be put in size order (7)

26 A level of 10 across sets one of these (9)

27 You would need a double blind experiment to control for this (12, 4)

31 The people who are used in a study (8)

35 Groups that have the same performance on 40 across (7)

37 In this type of relationship, as one variable increases the other decreases (8)

38 There is an equal distance between each point on this type of scale (8)
39 If your hypothesis predicts the direction of the effect you need this type of test (3, 6)
40 The part that is measured by the experimenter (9, 8)

DOWN
 1 The square root of 16 across (8, 9)
 2 Chance or likelihood (11)
 3 You need to do this to designs to control for small practice and fatigue effects (14)
 5 Another way of controlling for order effects (13)
 7 The parametric test for the independent groups design (11, 1, 4)
 8 See 11 down
 9 The non-parametric test for the repeated measures of matched groups design (8, 4)
11 and 8   This type of hypothesis does not predict the direction of the results (3, 6)
12 You add up all the scores and divide by the number of scores to get this (4)
13 The values of 10 across (6)
14 The consistency of a measure (11)
15 A bell-shaped symmetrical curve (6, 12)
18 Whether a measure measures what it is supposed to (8)
19 The non-parametric test for the independent groups design (4, 7)
22 A level at which the null hypothesis can be rejected (12)
23 and 24 No relationship (4, 11)
27 These types of tests require data that is 38 across (10)
28 The type of blind experiment in which subjects are kept unaware of the aim of the experiment (6)
30 These are types of 10 across that need to be controlled (9)
32 If the null hypothesis is rejected at the $p < 0.05$ level this means there is a $p > 0.95$ _____ level (10)
33 Frequency data is this (7)
34 The first word of a design in which the same subject's performance is measured under different conditions (8)
36 This scale has an absolute zero point (5)

SECTION TWO
METHODS OF INVESTIGATION

Combining evidence from different types of investigations

Psychology uses many different methods of investigation, each with its own advantages and disadvantages.

This section demonstrates different types of studies related to one topic. As you use the evidence in different ways you will learn some of the advantages and disadvantages. The section will also demonstrate how different types of evidence can be combined to support an argument. The topic to which all the investigations are related is the question of whether or not violence in the media (TV and films) is a cause of aggression in society.

Evidence from a number of psychological investigations suggests that there is a link between media violence and aggression. Broadcasters, however, know that violent films attract a large audience so they have a vested interest in keeping the violence on the screens.

Broadcasters' viewpoint	Concerned viewer
'Anyway, it earns us a lot of money.'	'Anyway, media violence frightens me.'

All this talk about TV causing aggression is based on flimsy evidence. I think people should be able to choose what they want to see.

There is considerable evidence from a number of different studies that TV violence causes aggression in society. The broadcasters have a responsibility to protect society.

For each piece of evidence that is presented you will be asked to take the view of either the broadcasters or the concerned viewers. Usually this will mean using the evidence given to support the view of the viewers, and criticising the evidence to support the broadcasters' view.

Each method of investigation is described and a table gives the advantages and disadvantages of that method. This is followed by one example of how this method has been used to provide evidence for the debate. In composing your arguments to support each viewpoint you should try to combine the evidence in the example with the advantages and disadvantages of the method.

As well as the specific advantages and disadvantages of each method of investigation, also keep in mind these more general issues:

- How true-to-life is the study?
- Is the sample representative of the general population or just part of the population?
- How far can the results of the study be generalised?

Laboratory experiment

In the experimental method subjects are put under different conditions and then their performance is measured. The laboratory is a convenient setting for the experimental method because the experimenter is able to control what happens.

Advantages	Disadvantages
1 Experimenter is able to control the experiences of the subjects, thus it is possible to isolate cause and effect relationships.	1 The laboratory is an artificial situation – because of this the subjects may act differently from the way they would in real life.
2 Equipment can be ready and available for measuring the subjects' behaviour.	2 The tasks set may have limited relevence to real life.
	3 The experiment only measures behaviour over a short period.

74

Example

Bandura, Ross and Ross (1963) studied the effects of observing aggression on the later aggressive behaviour of children. 96 children, with an average age of 4 years 4 months, were divided into four equal groups. Three groups were shown aggressive acts and then tested for their level of aggression. The fourth group acted as a control, not observing any aggressive acts. All children were studied individually.

The three experimental groups observed the same aggressive acts under different conditions. The conditions differed in who modelled the behaviour: one group observed an adult model in the same room; one group observed a film of an adult model; and the last group observed a cartoon model on TV being aggressive.

In each case the model was observed being aggressive to a 'Bobo' doll (ie a blow up doll weighted at the bottom so that it can stand up on its own). The model carried out the following sequence three times:

- sat on the doll and punched it in the nose repeatedly;
- stood the doll up and hit it over the head with a mallet;
- threw it up into the air;
- finally kicked it round the room.

While carrying out these acts the model said such things as 'Sock him in the nose . . .', 'Hit him down . . .', 'Throw him in the air . . .', and 'Kick him . . .'.

In the testing phase of the study each child was mildly frustrate by the experimenter explaining that the toys in one room were special toys reserved for other children, but the child was free to play with any of the toys in the other room. The other room contained a Bobo doll and a selection of aggressive toys (eg gun, mallet), and non-aggressive toys (eg tea set). The children's behaviour in this room was observed through a one-way mirror for 20 minutes. The behaviour was observed and recorded in five-second units. Table 10.1 summarises the results:

Observed behaviour	Type of model			
	Real-life adult	Filmed adult	Cartoon	Control (no model)
Average total aggression	82.9	91.5	99	54.3
Average imitation of aggression towards doll	21.3	16.4	12	5.7

Table 10.1 (Figures are mean number of 5 second units)

Reference

Bandura A, Ross D, and Ross AR (1963) 'Imitation of film-mediated aggressive models' *Journal of Abnormal and Social Psychology*, 66, 3–11.

Questions

1 How many subjects were used?

2 What was the average age of the subjects?

3 What were the conditions of the experiment? (There are four altogether.)

4 What measures (dependent variables) are shown in the table for each group?

5 Which group was the most aggressive overall?

6 Which group imitated aggression the most?

7 Write a paragraph using this evidence to support the view of the anti-media violence lobby.

8 Write a paragraph that uses the criticisms of the laboratory experiment and the evidence above to support the broadcasters' view.

Case study

This method is an in-depth study of one particular individual. Case studies are often carried out on people who are of special interest because they are outstanding or abnormal. Case studies can also be used to illustrate 'normal' behaviour or development.

Advantages

1 The case can be viewed in depth and long sequences of behaviour can be followed.

2 It is not artificial as it relates to one individual's real-life experiences.

Disadvantages

1 Being a study of only one person the results cannot be generalised as they may not be representative of the general population.

2 Often, case studies are carried out retrospectively (historically), and the evidence may become distorted in people's memories.

3 Cause and effect relationships are difficult to establish.

Example

In 1977 Ronald Zamora (aged 15) killed his 82-year-old next door neighbour, Elinor Haggart, who disturbed him while he was breaking into her home. She warned Zamora and his friend that she would call the police and Zamora shot her. Zamora confessed to the shooting, but in court his defence attorney pleaded that he was insane at the time of the murder because he 'acted under the influence of prolonged, intense, involuntary, subliminal television intoxication'. The attorney argued that commercials can influence anybody to buy products; similarly, watching programmes with murders can influence a person if they are in a similar situation to what is depicted on the screen. The court had to decide whether Zamora was sane at the time of the murder from the evidence provided by psychologists and psychiatrists who had interviewed the boy and his parents.

Zamora's parents described him as a TV addict. He watched an average of 6 hours a day, with a taste for cops and robbers programmes. His hero was Kojak and he had even asked his father to shave his head for him so that he would look more like his hero.

One psychiatrist said that the boy had compared the situation to an episode in Kojak where women had been shot and got up and walked away. Another said that Zamora sometimes pretended to be a good guy and sometimes a bad guy, and that he wished the shooting 'had been like a TV show where the dead get up when the show is over'. Dr Helen Ackerman described Zamora as being emotionally disturbed and unpredictable and noted that he had previously attempted to commit suicide and used to throw knives in the air and stand underneath them.

When asked the question 'Did TV teach you to kill anybody' Zamora replied 'No'. He also told another psychologist that the only thing that he had learned on TV was that the bad guys don't get away with it. Zamora himself did not blame TV for the murder, but there was evidence that he did imitate TV characters.

The jury decided that Zamora was sane at the time of the murder as he knew right from wrong and he knew the nature of the consequences of his act. He was convicted of the murder, the burglary and carrying a weapon and was given a life sentence.

Reference

Liebert RM and Sprafkin S (1988) *The early window: Effects of TV violence on children and youth* Pergamon.

Questions

1 How many subjects were used?

2 How old was Zamora?

3 What sources of evidence were used to compile the case study presented to the court?

4 What other sources of evidence might have been useful to get a clearer picture of his personality?

5 Apart from the method used, how does the evidence from this case study differ from the evidence provided by the Bandura, Ross and Ross experiment?

6 Write a paragraph that uses the criticisms of case studies to support the broadcasters' view.

7 Write a paragraph that uses the evidence of the case study to support the view of the anti-media violence lobby.

Field study

Field studies are investigations conducted outside the laboratory.

Advantages

1 More natural setting. This means that the subject's behaviour may be less affected by the study.

2 Subjects different from the ones that volunteer for laboratory experiments.

Disadvantages

1 It is difficult to control events that might affect a subject's behaviour.

2 Situations in which controlled studies can be conducted are rare and when found often have an abnormal population.

Example

Leyens *et al* (1975) investigated the effects of a week of either violent or neutral films on behaviour in a Belgian remand institution for secondary school boys. The institution consisted of four cottages which varied in the number of boys (16, 18, 19 and 32). Each cottage was run as a separate home by three or four trained counsellors. In all cottages TV viewing was strictly limited, and during the study the TVs were turned off. The researchers were able to investigate the effects of films without TV content interfering with their results.

Five trained observers were used. Four of them were randomly assigned to cottages, and the fifth rotated round the four to ensure consistency. The observers were placed in the cottages a week before the study so that they could get to know the boys and the boys could feel relaxed in their presence.

The study lasted three weeks. In the first week the observers rated the behaviour of the boys. The results found that there were two highly aggressive (HA) and two low level aggressive (LA) cottages.

The second week was movie week. Each cottage had a film every evening, which all the boys watched. One HA and one LA cottage were shown violent films, and the other two cottages were shown neutral/non-violent films. The violent films included *Bonnie and Clyde, The Dirty Dozen* and *Zorro*. The neutral films included *Lily, Daddy's Fiancee* and *La Belle Americaine*. The boys were observed throughout the movie week and the following week. Figure 10.1 shows the rated aggressiveness for the first and second weeks of the study.

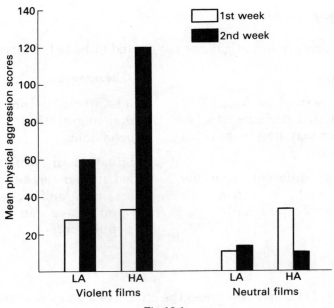

Fig 10.1

In the third week the boys in the HA cottage that had seen violent films continued to be more aggressive than they had been in the first week of the study. The other three groups returned to normal levels of aggression. One complication that occurred was that in the LA cottage that saw the violent films, a major fight broke out on the second day of movie week. The researchers were not sure how the punishment given by the counsellors affected the behaviour of this group.

Reference

Leyens J, Camino L, Parke RD, and Berkowitz L (1975) 'Effects of movie violence on aggression in a field setting as a function of group dominance and cohesion' *Journal of Personality and Social Psychology* 32, 346–360.

Questions

1 How many subjects were used in the study?

2 Why is it that this study could be carried out in an institution, but not on a housing estate?

3 What advantages would there be to carrying out a similar study on a housing estate (if it were possible)?

4 Which group increased the most in aggressiveness?

5 Write a short paragraph supporting the broadcasters' point of view, in which they defend themselves against the evidence provided by this study.

6 Write a short paragraph using the evidence from this study to support the anti-media violence lobby.

Longitudinal correlational study

This method follows the behaviour and development of a number of individuals over a long period. Longitudinal studies can be experimental, comparing groups who are treated differently over a long period of time. More often they use the correlational method, ie they look for a relationship between two or more variables (things that can be measured).

Advantages

1 It provides a record of the subjects' behaviour over a long period of time and therefore tends to be more reliable.

2 It is not artificial as it relates to real-life experiences.

Disadvantages

1 Because it takes a long period, there may be changes in society or the person's life that affect their behaviour.

2 Correlational studies can only tell us that there is a relationship between two variables. This relationship could be a causal one, but the relationship may also be caused by a third variable that affects both of the variables measured.

Example

Eron *et al* (1972) investigated the aggressive behaviour and TV viewing preferences of a group of 8 to 9-year-old children, and followed up some of the sample ten years later on.

In the first part of the study the entire population of 8 to 9-year-olds in a semi-rural town were selected for study – 875 in all. The mothers were asked to name the child's three favourite TV programmes. Each of these programmes was then rated as either violent or

81

non-violent. The researchers then interviewed each of the children separately about how aggressive the other children were. From these interviews they were able to rate the children on peer-rated aggression, ie how aggressive their peers thought they were.

The results of this first part of the study showed a strong positive correlation between preference for violent TV and level of peer-rated aggression.

Ten years later, in the second part of the study, 427 of the original sample, now aged 18–19, were contacted. Each was asked what their three favourite TV programmes were, and their peers were interviewed about their level of aggression. In contrast to the findings in the earlier part of the study there was not a positive correlation between a preference for violent TV and peer-rated aggression.

The long-term comparison for the subjects studied at both ages found that there was a strong correlation between a preference for violent TV at age 8–9, and peer-rated aggression at 18–19 years. However, there was no relationship between a preference for violent TV at 18–19 years and peer-rated aggression at 8–9 years of age.

Eron *et al* suggested that a likely interpretation of the evidence was that viewing violent TV at the age of 8–9 had long-term effects on aggressive behaviour. At 8–9 years the children copy the aggressive acts and this becomes part of their personality.

Reference

Eron LE, Heusmann LR, Leftkowitz MM and Walder LO (1972) 'Does television cause aggression?' *American Psychologist*, 27, 253–263.

Questions

1 How many subjects were used in the long-term comparison?

2 How was preference for violent TV measured at age 8–9?

3 How was preference for violent TV measured at age 18–19?

4 Why might the measure of peer-rated aggression be more accurate than asking parents or teachers to rate the subjects aggression levels?

5 Summarise the results of the study in a table similar to the one below:

Measures	Relationship/no relationship
Preference for violent TV age 8–9 and peer-rated aggression age 8–9	_____
Preference for violent TV age 18–19 and peer-rated aggression age 8–9	_____
Preference for violent TV age 18–19 and peer-rated aggression age 18–19	_____
Preference for violent TV age 8–9 and peer-rated aggression age 18–19	_____

6 Write a short paragraph using the criticisms of correlation studies to support the broadcasters' view.

7 Combine evidence from Bandura and Walters, the case study and Eron's study to support the view of the anti-media violence lobby.

Cross-cultural studies

A culture is a way of life, and this may affect behaviour. Cross-cultural studies look at the same behaviours, processes, or relationships in different cultures to find out if they are the same or different.

Advantages

1 They allow behaviour to be viewed in a wider context.

2 They can determine whether behaviours or relationships are unique to one culture or not.

Disadvantages

1 There are great difficulties in ensuring that the measures taken are fair to, or relevant for, each culture.

2 Cultures vary in many different ways and it is difficult to identify which are the important ways in which they differ and which are unimportant.

Example

Heusmann and Eron (1986) reported the findings of seven similar longitudinal studies carried out in Australia, Finland, France, Holland, Poland and the USA. All the studies used the same measures of behaviour and TV viewing (apart from Holland, where the measures varied slightly), and all studied the relationship between the amount of violence viewed on TV and the level of aggression in 7 to 9-year-old children. These studies were then considered together as a cross-cultural study.

In all of the cultures studied there was a relationship between the amount of violence viewed by children and their level of aggression. This overall finding was, however, affected by a number of mediating factors.

One important mediating factor was the degree to which violence was accepted and used by parents and friends. This was most clearly seen in Israel where there was a comparison between children who lived in a Kibbutz and city children. (A kibbutz is a communal village which lives to a large extent separately from the outside world. Good relations between the members of the kibbutz are encouraged through sharing property and the work necessary for living.) Children living in a kibbutz showed no relation between aggression ratings and the amount of TV violence viewed. City children, however, showed the strongest correlation found in all of the seven studies.

Overall measures of how violent the society was and how much violence was shown on television in each society produced the results shown in Table 10.2.

Culture	Overall level of aggression	Aggressive content of TV
AUSTRALIA	relatively low	medium
FRANCE	relatively low	medium
FINLAND	low	low
HOLLAND	relatively low	medium
ISRAEL	medium	medium
POLAND	low	relatively low
USA	high	high

Table 10.2

Reference

Heusmann LR, and Eron LD (1986) *Television and the Aggressive Child: A Cross National Comparison* Lawrence Earlbaum, London.

Questions

1 What age were the subjects?

2 Plot the information in the table on a graph like Figure 2b:

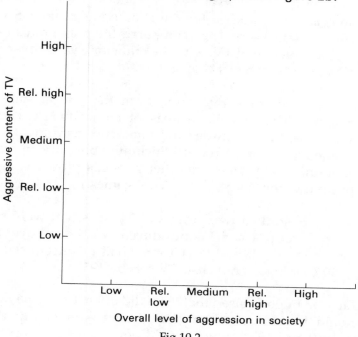

Fig 10.2

3 What type of correlation is it?

4 Write a paragraph criticising the evidence, to support the broadcasters' view.

5 Write a paragraph using this evidence to support the anti-media violence lobby. Point out what implications this study has for other studies that you have looked at.

Natural experiments

Natural experiments take advantage of a naturally-occurring change in society. By measuring before and after the change the experimenter hopes to find out what affect the change had on society. The change takes the role of the independent variable in the experiment.

Advantages	Disadvantages
1 Behaviour is observed in completely natural surroundings.	1 There is no control over other changes that might occur.
2 The samples are usually large and include a wide cross section of the population.	2 The measure may be more inaccurate than direct observation.

85

Example

Hennigan *et al* (1982) studied the effect on crime in the USA of the introduction of television. They compared the crime rates in cities before the introduction of TV, with the crime rate when over 50% of households in the city had TV sets.

Their measures of crime rate came from the official statistics of reported crime. The two main areas of crime investigated were violent crime, including murder and rape, and instrumental crime, ie crime aimed at gaining a reward, including burglary and larceny. (Larceny is unlawfully taking another person's property, eg shop-lifting, pickpocketing, forgery, and 'con' games.)

The researchers studied two groups of 34 cities that were roughly equal in size. Group A had TV introduced in 1949 and over 50% of households had TV sets by 1951. Group B had TV introduced in 1953 and over 50% of households had TV sets by 1955.

Hennigan *et al* hypothesised that if TV did affect the crime rate then they should be able to observe an increase in Group A cities between 1949 and 1952, which would not occur in Group B cities. Also they should be able to observe an increase in crime rate in Group B cities between 1953 and 1956 that would bring them in line with the crime rates in Group A cities.

The results indicated no consistent increase in violent crimes, but there was a consistent increase in larceny that coincided with the introduction of TV in both Group A and Group B cities. This increase in larceny was surprising as it is a crime that is rarely portrayed on the TV, so it is unlikely that the increase is due to people copying the crime. The researchers suggested that the increase might be explained by the effect of advertising increasing a need for consumer goods. If people are continually exposed to images of a lifestyle that is richer than theirs, some members of the audience may decide to acquire these consumer goods by criminal means.

The researchers noted that it is difficult to compare this study to the effects of TV nowadays because the content of TV is different. TV is generally more realistic in its portrayal of crime than it was in the 1950s. The study is also limited because it only looked at levels of reported crime.

Reference

Hennigan KM, Del Rosario ML, Heath L, Cook TD, Wharton JD, and Calder BJ (1982) 'Impact of Introduction of Television on Crime in the United States: Empirical Findings and Theoretical Implications' *Journal of Personality and Social Psychology* 42, 461–477.

Questions

1 What was the independent variable?

2 What was the dependent variable?

3 Between 1949 and 1952 which group was the control group?

4 Between 1953 and 1956 which group was the control group?

5 Why was it important for the researchers to find an increase in crime in both Group A and Group B cities?

6 Why might the official statistics of reported crime be an inaccurate measure of the actual level of violence in society?

7 Write a paragraph using the evidence to support the broadcasters' views.

8 Write a paragraph criticising the evidence to support the views of the anti-media violence lobby.

SECTION THREE
PRACTICALS

Note

Throughout this section the guidelines for analysis of the results have purposefully been kept to a minimum. This is because the exact analysis necessary for each practical will depend on how you measure the dependent variable, and the characteristics of the data provided by your practical.

In general you should aim to use as many descriptive statistics as possible (ie averages, measures of spread and graphs). To report a practical well you will often have to try out different ways of presenting your data in rough, before you choose the best summary to use in the results section.

1 The horizontal-vertical illusion

Background

Illusions provide psychologists with interesting theoretical problems. The Horizontal-Vertical Illusion (HVI) has received quite a lot of attention. The illusion is that horizontal and vertical lines of equal length often do not appear to be the same length (Figure 1a).

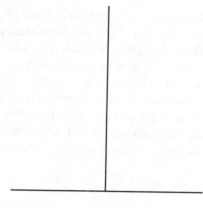

Fig 1a

The effect of the illusion can be demonstrated using pen and paper tests in which the subject is asked to adjust the lengths of lines so that they appear equal in length.

The explanation that is most often given is that vertical lines are perceived as longer than horizontal lines, ie the length of the vertical line is overestimated (McBride, Risser and Slotnick, 1987).

The illusion could occur for other reasons. One alternative explanation is that the horizontal line is apparently shortened by the bisection of the vertical line. Finger and Spelt (1947), for example, found that subjects adjusted a vertical line much less when the figure was an L-shape, as opposed to the usual inverted T (as above).

Verillo and Irvin (1979) found that the illusion did not occur if the figures were presented in a darkened room. However, they observed that estimates for the lengths of vertical lines did not differ between the dark condition (no contextual cues) and the light condition (contextual cues), but horizontal lines were judged to be shorter in the light condition than the dark condition.

McBride, Risser, and Slotnick (1987) concluded that the illusion is due to the combined effects of the bisection shortening the horizontal line and an overestimation of the vertical line. They confirmed the findings of Finger and Spelt (1947) and found that when subjects were asked to draw a one-inch line accurately, they could draw horizontal lines fairly accurately, but consistently overestimated the lengths of the vertical lines that they drew (ie they consistently drew vertical lines shorter than horizontal lines).

A number of studies include evidence that experience affects a person's susceptibility to the illusion. In a study in Africa, Segall, Campbell and Harkowits (1966) found that the magnitude of the illusion was greater for people who lived on the plain than it was for those who lived in restricted environments. Becker (1972) found that the effect was reduced if the subjects were made aware of the effect. Fraisse and Vantrey (1956) found that the effect was greater for social science students than science students, but McBride *et al* (1987) found no difference between social science and architecture undergraduates.

Keywords

Illusions; perception; cross-cultural studies and the nature-nurture of perception.

Bibliography

McBride SA, Risser JM and Slotnick (1987) 'The Horizontal Vertical Illusion: Independence of Line Bisection and a Comparison Line'. *Perceptual and Motor Skills*, 64, 943–948.

Possible methods

A partial replication of the tests conducted by McBride *et al* (1987) would be easiest to conduct:

1 Ask subjects to draw ten one-inch lines (five vertical and five horizontal) on separate pieces of paper. Compare lengths of lines.

   and/or

2 Compare the magnitude of the effect for inverted T and L-shapes. Copy Figures 1b and 1c opposite and present them on separate pieces of paper. Give the subject a piece of card and

ask them to cover the vertical line so that it is the same length as the horizontal line, and then mark this with a pencil. Measure the lengths of lines and compare.

and/or

3 Compare different groups of students, eg social science vs engineering.

Note: When a repeated measures design is used it is worth considering counterbalancing the order of presentation.

Variations

- Does the effect occur if Figures 1b and 1c are inverted?

- Is the bisection effect measurable? Can this be measured by getting subjects to adjust the length of bisected and unbisected horizontal lines? Or will the bisection effect occur in a production task where the subject is asked to produce one-inch horizontal lines that are either bisected or unbisected?

- Does the effect occur in the construction of a square? Devise an apparatus in which the subject has to adjust the height and width of a rectangle to make a square, and then measure the height and width produced. Or get subjects to draw squares, either freehand or using plain straight-edges.

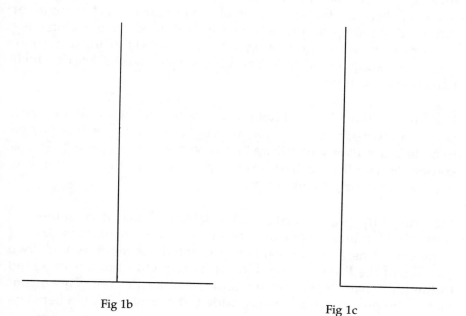

Fig 1b

Fig 1c

2 Figure ground reversal

Background

When viewing pictures we often interpret them as though they have depth. This is an illusion: pictures are two-dimensional and we *imagine* the third dimension of depth.

At the beginning of the century Gestalt psychologists investigated the ways in which we organise our perception of pictorial representations. One of the most basic organisations observed was that we divide the picture into figure and ground. The figure is the part that is perceived to have a 'thing like' quality, and the ground is the background to the figure.

This figure-ground organisation was first investigated in detail by Rubin (1921). He noted that the figure had form and shape, whereas the ground was formless, and that the figure also appeared to be nearer than the ground.

If the figure does appear to be nearer than the ground, how does the brain change the qualities of that part of a picture to make it differ from the ground?

To investigate this type of question psychologists have often used reversible figures such as *Rubin's vase*. These pictures are said to be reversible because the same parts of the picture can act as figure or ground depending on the way in which it is perceived. Originally these pictures were used along with the method of introspection. They were shown to a subject and the subject had to describe their perceptions in detail.

Early research (eg Fry and Robertson, 1935) established that when a part of a reversible picture was perceived to be a figure it appeared to be brighter than when it was perceived to be the ground. This is consistent with the fact that closer objects appear brighter and this is used as a cue for judging distance.

More recently Brigner (1986) has established that if brightness is controlled for, an area of a picture will appear to increase in size if it is perceived as a figure. Brigner presented his subjects with two pictures of the Rubin's vase. One of these pictures had eyes added to the faces part of the picture, and the other did not. This meant that in the picture with the eyes added, the white space in between

94

the two faces was likely to be seen as ground. In the other, untouched picture the white space was likely to be perceived as a figure, ie a vase. Brigner asked eight subjects to make a comparison between the size of the white space in both pictures. All eight subjects judged the white spaces of the vase to be bigger than the white space of the background to the two faces.

Keywords

Perception; reversible figures; depth/distance cues; ambiguous figures/drawings; illusions

Bibliography

Brigner WL (1986) 'Change in perceived size with Figure-Ground reversal' *Perceptual and Motor Skills*, 63, 254.
Haber RN and Hershenson M (1980) *The Psychology of Visual Perception*. (2nd ed.) Holt, Rinehart and Winston: London.

Possible methods

A replication of Brigner (1986) would be possible, using the two versions of Rubin's vase on page 96.

1 Copy the figures on to two sheets. Present them to subjects at the same distance and brightness. (If possible, measure brightness with a spot meter on a camera.) Counterbalance left and right presentation.

2 Explain to subjects: *Notice that the white space can be perceived as the space between two faces with white eyes, or it can be perceived as a vase. I want you to make a judgement about the size of the white space. Is the white space between the two faces with white eyes larger or is the vase larger?*

Analysis

Graphical/binomial test

Variations

- A confirmation of Fry's (1935) finding could be sought by using the above method, and ensuring that the brightness is the same for the two diagrams. Ask subjects which white space appears brighter.

● Can any other reversible figures be investigated in this way?

3 Memory for pictorial advertising

Background

Advertisers have in the past used information from research that did not particularly relate to advertising to guide them in their presentation of a product. Recent research has been more specific and looked directly at the link between memory and advertising.

One of the main reasons for a company advertising a product is to increase market awareness of that product. Therefore an important issue in advertising is how easy it is to recall a particular advertisement. Companies hope that their brand names will be recalled when the product is needed.

Advertisements in printed materials (eg newspapers, *Yellow pages*) often present the brand name and product as a pictorial image. This is consistent with laboratory memory research which suggests that visual memory is often superior to verbal memory (eg Paivio, 1969).

Lippman and Shannan (1973) suggested that in advertising which promotes a new, or unfamiliar, brand name and product pair, the memory test should be considered similar to a paired-associate task. The critical feature of the advert is the association between the brand name and the product. A question then arises as to what is the best way to combine brand name and product with a picture?

Lutz and Lutz (1977) chose brand product pairs that were depicted in various pictorial forms in the *Yellow pages* of a telephone directory. Their results suggested that an interactive pictorial presentation is the best way to encourage people to recall brand product information.

Interactive relationship

Pictorial   *Letter accentuation*

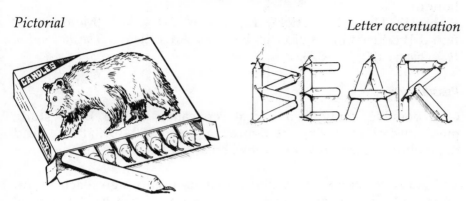

Non-interactive relationship

Pictorial   *Letter accentuation*

Adapted from Esser *et al* (1986)

Esser *et al* (1986) confirmed the findings of Lutz and Lutz in a more controlled experiment. They further found that interactive pictorial presentation was more easily recalled than interactive letter accentuation, and that pictorial presentation was superior to letter accentuation.

Keywords

Recall; paired-associate recall; dual coding

Bibliography

Baddeley AD (1976) *The Psychology of Memory* Harper and Row, London.
Esser JK, Die AH, Seholm KJ, Pebley SR (1986) 'Memory for Brand-Product information in Pictorial Advertising' *The Journal of Psychology*, 120, 363–373.

Possible methods

One possible study is a partial replication of the Esser study mentioned above, using the figures on pages 100–109. (These need to be photocopied and, if possible, enlarged.)

The study would be an independent groups design, each group presented with 20 brand-product pairs on flashcards. Esser *et al* used a presentation rate of ten seconds per advert.

The conditions would be: Group A = interactive pictures; Group B = non-interactive pictures.

The response can be either free recall (where the subjects are asked to recall the brand-product pairs in any order without any cues to recall) or paired associate (with the product given, eg matches, and the subject asked to recall the brand – Lion). See page 115 for a prepared response sheet.

It would be more realistic if there was a delay, with a distraction task between presentation and recall – as we do not often see an advertisement and immediately walk into a shop.

Analysis

Graphical/test of difference comparing number of pairs recalled.

Similarly, responses interactive or non-interactive pictures could be compared with plain words.

NB The brand-product pairs presented on pages 100–109 were prepared following the outlines provided by Esser *et al* (1986): a) Common nouns and no proper nouns, b) pairs could not rhyme, c) pairs could not be alliterative, d) pairs could not suggest one another, e) pairs do not actually exist, and f) both had to be able to be pictorially represented.

98

Variations

- A selection of real adverts from the *Yellow pages* which showed the characteristics of interactive pictures and interactive letters could be used.

- Does the same effect occur if the adverts are presented on video?

- What causes most interference with the memory: the brand name associated with another product, or different brand names associated with the same product?

Non-interactive pictures

FOREST
LAMPS

DEVIL
CARPETS

DORMOUSE
BEDS

SERPENT
CARS

**GLOBE
BUCKETS**

**LIME
RECORDS**

**PHEASANT
SHOES**

**STRAWBERRY
BOOKS**

LEAF
CURTAINS

FOX
TABLES

PENCIL
WIGS

SHEEP
LOCKS

102

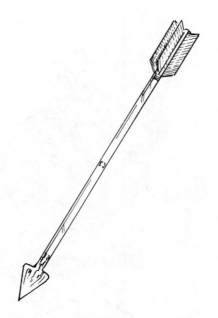

ARROW
SCALES

ELEPHANT
WINDOWS

UMBRELLA
TEAPOTS

STAR
HATS

STORK TYPEWRITERS

GOBLIN BATHS

GIRAFFE SUNROOFS

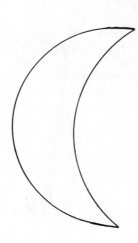

MOON PLUGS

104

Interactive pictures

**FOREST
LAMPS**

**DEVIL
CARPETS**

**DORMOUSE
BEDS**

**SERPENT
CARS**

**GLOBE
BUCKETS**

**LIME
RECORDS**

**PHEASANT
SHOES**

**STRAWBERRY
BOOKS**

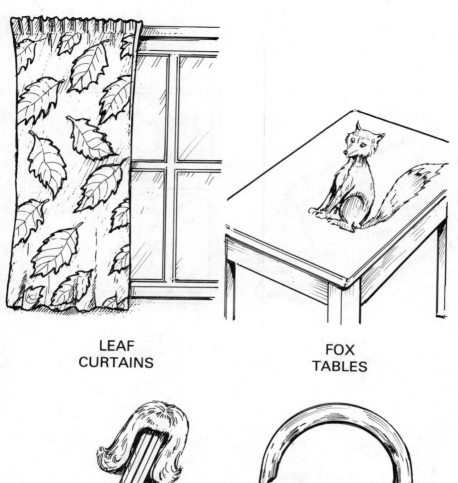

**LEAF
CURTAINS**

**FOX
TABLES**

**PENCIL
WIGS**

**SHEEP
LOCKS**

**ARROW
SCALES**

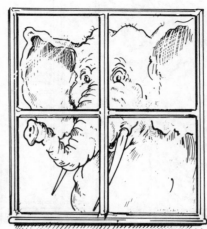

**ELEPHANT
WINDOWS**

**UMBRELLA
TEAPOTS**

**STAR
HATS**

**STORK
TYPEWRITERS**

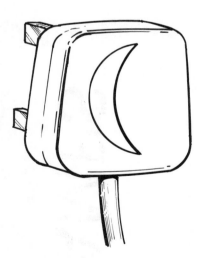

**GOBLIN
BATHS**

**GIRAFFE
SUNROOFS**

**MOON
PLUGS**

CARPETS

CARS

LAMPS

BEDS

BUCKETS RECORDS

SHOES BOOKS

111

CURTAINS   TABLES

WIGS   LOCKS

112

WINDOWS

HATS

SCALES

TEAPOTS

BATHS

PLUGS

TYPEWRITERS

SUNROOFS

114

Paired Associate Response Sheet

Please fill in as many of the missing brand names as you can:

_____ LAMPS

_____ CARPETS

_____ BEDS

_____ CARS

_____ BUCKETS

_____ RECORDS

_____ SHOES

_____ BOOKS

_____ CURTAINS

_____ TABLES

_____ WIGS

_____ LOCKS

_____ SCALES

_____ WINDOWS

_____ TEAPOTS

_____ HATS

_____ TYPEWRITERS

_____ BATHS

_____ SUNROOFS

_____ PLUGS

4 Question order and eye-witness testimony

Background

A person who witnesses a crime or an accident may be asked by police or insurance companies to provide evidence. This often means that they need to recall the events some time after they occurred. The witness is set a complex, long-term memory task in which he or she has to remember details of people's appearance and behaviour.

Since early research by Stern (1904) the inaccuracies of eye-witness testimony have been well documented. Documenting the inaccuracies enables psychologists to warn the police and the courts about relying too heavily on eye-witness accounts. But it does not tackle the more practical question of what is the best way to get information from an eye witness?

Tulving and Pearlstone (1966) demonstrated that a person's memory for words could be improved by giving them retrieval cues, ie cues that help them access the information in the memory. These and similar experiments (eg Tulving and Osler, 1968), have shown that cued memory for lists of words is superior to free recall. If these studies on words can be generalised to memories for events it suggests that careful questioning of a witness might be more effective than simply asking them to give a statement.

Schank and Abelson (1977) suggested that a person's memory for an experience can be organised in the form of 'scripts' or 'schemas'. Schank (1982) further suggested that reminding subjects of the main events of an experience, which would have been processed in more detail, would aid recall of other details. In relation to a crime these main events may be the main characters or the crime itself.

Alternatively, the memory for an experience may be encoded in a way that reflects the time sequence of the original experience. Bekerian and Bowers (1983) found that misleading questions could distort memory in a pictorial recognition task, but this distortion could be overcome if the pictorial recognition test followed the order of the original experience.

Malpass and Devine (1981) demonstrated that a subject's memory for a staged act of vandalism could be improved by reminding the subject of the main events and exploring their memory for their

116

feelings at the time. However Loftus *et al*'s (1983) study, in which subjects viewed a stressfull film of a hospital fire found that recall was impaired by reminding the subjects of the fire and what the hospital looked like before the fire.

Morris and Morris (1985) investigated the effect of question order on accuracy of recall. Combining the suggestions of Schank (1982) and the findings of Bekerian and Bowers (1983) and Loftus *et al* (1983), they hypothesised that question orders that reflected the organisation of memory scripts should be more effective than question orders that do not. They suggested that memory for an experience would be more likely to be organised in a time sequence or around · the major characters than around the major event (the crime or accident).

In their experiment, subjects were shown a video sequence depicting a chase and then a crime. After watching this, each subject was asked to write an account of the film. They were then asked 25 questions about details relating to the people in the film (eg What colour shirt? What was the name of . . .?), and their actions (eg Who pulled a gun first? Who bumped into the dustbins?). These questions were the same for all subjects but presented in a different order.

The results showed that question orders which followed the time sequence of the film, or asked questions about the central characters first, were more effective than a random sequence of questions or when questions were asked about the main event first. The most significant finding was that the ordering of the questions that followed the time sequence of the film was almost 20 percent better than randomly ordered questions (Morris and Morris, 1985).

Keywords

Eye-witness reports; memory; question order; retrieval cues.

Bibliography

Morris V and Morris PE (1985) 'The influence of question order on eyewitness accuracy' *British Journal of Psychology*, 76, 365–371.
Gardiner M (1976) *Readings in Human Memory*. Methuen, London.

Possible methods

A partial replication of Morris and Morris (1985) could be carried out as follows:

1 Videotape a TV crime drama, or rent a video from a local video store and select a five-minute sequence that depicts scenes leading up to a main event such as a chase or a shooting.

2 Devise 20 questions, ten relating to the central characters and ten to the main events. (Other questions relating to non-important characters could also be added.)

3 Use an independent groups design. Give Group A the questions in the order that the events occur in the film. Give Group B questions in a random order. Compare the number of questions answered correctly.

(NB Morris and Morris (1985) asked subjects to write an account of the film and then gave them the questions. This could be omitted or included.)

Analysis

Graphical; test of difference between number of correctly-answered questions.

A more complex comparison could be made to find out whether the question-order effect lasts over time, comparing recall soon after viewing with recall a day after viewing.

Also, as there are copyright problems involved in showing videos in colleges, a more naturalistic study could be arranged. Choose a programme that you know that a lot of fellow students watch, develop the questionnaire and then seek subjects that watched the programme. Although this would be more natural there would be more uncontrolled factors.

Variations

Similar studies could test to see whether the question-order effect works for film sequences that do not lead up to a main event such as a crime, or for sequences in which the main event occurs first and it is the following events that need to be recalled. (The material does not have to be a film, it could be a play or a lecture.)

5 The recency effect and the modality effect

Background

The recency effect refers to the finding that subjects are more likely to recall the last couple of items on a list than items in the middle of a list. This effect was first noted by Ebbinghaus (see Figure 5a).

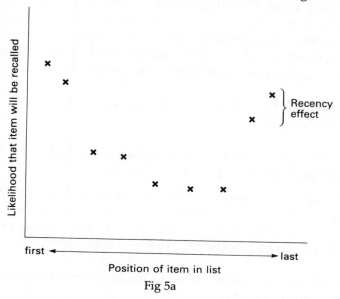

Fig 5a

Investigations in the 1960s found that the recency effect was most noticeable if auditory presentation was used. If items were presented visually then the recency effect was either absent or very weak (Corballis, 1966). The fact that the recency effect only occurs for auditory presentation is known as the modality effect.

The modality effect has been demonstrated in a number of experiments using different conditions of recall:

Immediate free recall – items immediately recalled in any order (Craik, 1969);

Immediate serial recall – items immediately recalled in the order that they were presented (Conrad and Hull, 1968);

Delayed free recall – items recalled in any order after a short period of doing a silent distracter task (Routh and Mayes, 1974);

Delayed serial recall – items recalled in order of presentation after a short period of doing a silent distracter task (Broadbent *et al*, 1978).

119

One explanation for the modality effect has been that it reflects the operation of auditory sensory memory, also called echoic memory or pre-categorical acoustic storage (PAS); (Crowder and Morton, 1969). The PAS stores auditory information for a short period without processing that information; this means that the last couple of items on a list are accessible. This explanation finds support from studies that show that if an irrelevant sound (a stimulus suffix) followed the presentation of the last item the recency effect was greatly reduced (eg Crowder, 1967). The stimulus suffix is said to reduce the recency effect as the suffix dislodges the last item from the PAS and occupies the storage space itself.

More recent findings have questioned the PAS explanation of the modality effect:

- Campbell and Dodd (1980) found an enhanced recency effect in lists that had been lipread by subjects.

- Greene and Crowder (1984, 1986) found enhanced recency effects for visually presented items that were mouthed silently by the subjects. This was found in both free and serial recall and in both immediate and delayed conditions.

These findings have been obtained using different types of stimuli, eg digits, letters and short words.

These findings are said to question the PAS explanation for the modality effect as they have found enhanced recency effects for visually presented stimuli in ways that seem to exclude the use of the PAS. This does not necessarily mean that the PAS is not involved in the modality effect but it does suggest that the phenomenon is not fully understood.

Could the explanation lie in other sensory stores for articulation and visual movement? Could it be due to the link between articulatory and acoustic coding? Could it be that there are other extensions to the modality effect that have not been investigated?

Keywords

Short-term memory; recency effect; modality effect; echoic memory; pre-categorical acoustic stores (PAS); suffix effects

120

Bibliography

Greene RL and Crowder RG (1986) 'Recency Effects in Delayed Recall of Mouthed Stimuli' *Memory and Cognition*, 14, 355–360.

Possible methods

For all variations below:

Present lists of between 6–10 items using flashcards (or if you are lucky enough, a memory drum or computer), at a presentation rate of 2 seconds per item. The lists can be composed of digits, letters, or short words. See pages 167–169.

For the silent distracter task for a delayed recall condition prepare flashcards with simple equations, eg $1 + 2 = 3$. The subject has to decide whether they are correct or incorrect. If correct they tap desk with right hand, if incorrect tap with left hand. Greene and Crowder used a 40 second delay therefore 20 equations are needed.

If flashcards are being used, pseudo-randomisation can be produced by shuffling the cards before each trial.

It is probably advisable to discard the evidence for the first two trials as the subject needs time to adjust to the procedure.

Recall should be in the form of written answers by the subject.

1 Demonstration of recency effect:
Each subject is presented with a number of lists of items and asked to recall immediately (either serial or free recall). Likelihood of recall can then be plotted against item position.

2 Demonstration of modality effect:
Repeated measures design: Condition A – visual presentation (experimenter shows cards); Condition B – auditory presentation (experimenter reads cards). Each condition consists of a number of lists. Experimenter indicates to subject non-verbally when they can write down the list.

3 Demonstration of stimulus suffix effect:
Repeated measures design: Condition A – auditory presentation followed immediately by 'Please write now'; Condition B – auditory

presentation without suffix, ie non-verbal indication of when to write list.

4 Demonstration of effect of mouthing:
Repeated measures: Condition A – visual presentation, silently mouthed; Condition B – visual presentation, unmouthed.

Analysis

For 2, 3, and 4: graphs can be compared; test of difference between likelihood of recall of last item in both conditions.

Variations

What happens if subjects write the list beneath desk during presentation? In delayed recall what happens if the distracter task involves the subject silently mouthing stimuli?

---

6 Prosocial behaviour and touching

Background

Prosocial behaviour refers to helping behaviour, usually the helping of strangers. It has been a focus for research in Social Psychology since Latane and Darley's classic study *The Unresponsive Bystander* (1970) in which the researchers noted that helping behaviour was fairly rare.

Other research has focused on the conditions that promote prosocial behaviour. For example, Brian and Test (1967) found that people were more likely to help if they had recently seen someone helping in a similar situation, ie a helping model.

Touching strangers is relatively rare in western society as it is usually considered a sign of intimacy. Argyle (1984) reported that a number of American studies showed that women respond positively to being touched by women whereas men can respond negatively. Fisher, Rytting and Hesslin (1976) reported that female students gave higher ratings to female librarians after they had been 'accidentally' touched by them, whereas male students gave lower ratings after they had been touched.

122

Willis and Hamm (1980) demonstrated that being 'accidentally' touched led to greater compliance from subjects.

Where a person is touched is important. The areas of the body on which it is acceptable to be touched vary according to whether the touched person is male or female and also on the sex of the toucher (see Jourard (1966) in Argyle (1984)).

Studies investigating the effect of touch usually contain a touch condition and a no-touch control condition. The part of the body touched in these studies is most often the arm, closely followed by the shoulder and hand (Paulsell and Goldman, 1984). These areas are acceptable and innocuous as parts of the body to be touched; touching them does not greatly infringe the norms of acceptable behaviour.

Paulsell and Goldman (1984) investigated the relationship between the sex of the toucher and the touched, the part of the arm that was touched, and the incidence of helping behaviour. Male and female experimenters approached young adults in shopping arcades and asked them to answer questions for a survey. At the end of the interview the experimenter either touched the subjects shoulder, upper arm, lower arm, or hand, or did not touch the subject. The experimenter then immediately 'accidentally' dropped some survey forms and recorded whether or not the subject helped them to pick them up.

The results showed that overall female experimenters got more help than male experimenters, and received more help from males than females. Overall, greater help was received by all experimenters when the upper arm was touched, this being particularly true of female experimenters touching male subjects on the upper arm, where 90% helped. Male experimenters received the same amount of help from males and females in the touch conditions. In fact there was very little difference between the amount of help they received between the touch conditions and the no-touch control condition.

Paulsell and Goldman (1984) do not attempt to explain the 'sex' difference found in their study, but merely note that it is a variable that should be taken into account in further studies. Are the results explainable in terms of the different areas of the body that it is acceptable to touch? Are they explainable in terms of males being socialised to help females? (It is not clear from Paulsell and Goldman's study whether there was a sex difference in the no-touch control conditions.)

Keywords

Prosocial behaviour; altruism; bodily contact; body contract; touching behaviour

Bibliography

Argyle (1984) *The Psychology of Interpersonal Behaviour* Penguin, Harmondsworth.
Latane B and Darley JM (1970) *The Unresponsive Bystander: Why doesn't he help?* Prentice Hall, New Jersey.
Paulsell S and Goldman M (1984) 'The effect of Touching Different Body areas on Prosocial Behaviour', *The Journal of Social Psychology*, 122, 269–273.

Possible methods

A partial replication of Paulsell and Goldman (1984) could be conducted, investigating whether there is a sex difference in prosocial behaviour. Or investigation into whether the part of the body touched affects amount of help.

1 Use male and/or female experimenters with male and female subjects.

2 Compare conditions: Touch on upper arm vs touch on hand or Touch vs no-touch control (depending on aim of investigation).

Analysis

Graphical/test of goodness of fit for frequency of help.

Variations

• Compare the effects of Touch vs no-touch conditions on compliance to fill out a questionnaire. Subjects either touched or not on first approach, does this affect whether they will comply with request to fill in questionnaire? (see Willis and Hamm, 1980).

• Compare Touch vs no-touch conditions on length of answer given when asking for directions. One experimenter could approach the subject, either touching them or not, and ask for directions to a particular point in town, eg the Post Office, and another experimenter could time the interaction.

124

7 Personal space/interpersonal distance

Background

Personal space refers to the area around a person's body that they feel they need to keep free of other people in order to remain comfortable. As the term refers to the preferred distance between one person and another Long (1980) has suggested that we should use the term 'interpersonal distance preference'. Although this term is slightly more long-winded it is more descriptive as people do not usually feel uncomfortable if they are close to inanimate objects.

Argyle (1979, 1984) notes that interpersonal distance is often a sign of intimacy, with people with whom the subject is more intimate allowed closer than strangers. For strangers, the preferred distance varies with culture – North American and European cultures preferring a greater distance than Arab cultures. Status also affects interpersonal distance, and in some cases there are even prescribed distances to which people should keep, eg within the Indian caste system.

More recent research has demonstrated that if all the above factors are kept constant, interpersonal distance is also affected by environmental factors. Using a technique known as the 'stop' technique, in which the subject tells an approaching experimenter to stop when they feel that they are at a comfortable speaking distance, Cochran and Urbanczyk (1982) found that people preferred more distance in a room with a low ceiling than they did in a room with a high ceiling. Cochran *et al* (1984) further found that subjects needed less interpersonal distance to feel comfortable outdoors (mean distance 0.54 metres) than they did indoors (mean distance 0.73 metres).

These results have been explained in terms of an adaptation of Hall's (1966) Spheroid model of Personal Space. Hall suggested that the personal space requirements of a person extended all round their body roughly in the shape of a sphere. Cochran *et al* (1982, 1984) have suggested that there is a 'trade off' between vertical space and horizontal space. If space above a person's head (vertical space), is limited by a ceiling they require a greater distance from another person (horizontal space). (Think of personal space as being like a balloon – what happens when a balloon is squeezed?)

Long (1984) investigated the relationship between stress and interpersonal distance preference. He used pencil and paper measures in which subjects were asked to rate how relaxed they were on a scale of 1–7. They also indicated on a diagram where they would want people to stop for them to feel comfortable. Long found that the more tense the situation the greater the distance the subject preferred. He concluded that people use greater personal distance to moderate stress.

Keywords

Personal space; proximity; (need for affiliation)

Bibliography

Argyle M and Trower P (1979) *Person to Person* Harper and Row.
Argyle M (1984) *The Psychology of Interpersonal Behaviour* (4th ed.) Penguin, Harmondsworth.
Cochran CD, Hale WD, and Hissam CP (1984) 'Personal Space requirements in indoor versus outdoor locations', *The Journal of Psychology*, 117, 121–123.
Long GT (1984) 'Psychological Tension and Closeness to other: Stress and interpersonal distance'. *The Journal of Psychology*, 117, 143–146.

Possible methods

A replication of Cochran *et al*'s studies could be undertaken as follows:

1 Explain to the subject that the purpose of the study is to determine how near or how far apart people prefer to be to feel comfortable. Ask the subject to stand on a particular spot and approach them slowly from a distance of ten feet, and ask the subject to tell you to stop when your closeness begins to make them feel uncomfortable. Then measure the distance between yourself and the subject.

2 A repeated measures design could be used with the following conditions: high vs low ceiling (perhaps classroom vs hall) *or* indoors vs outdoors.

Analysis

Graphical/test of difference, or, if many different conditions are used, test of correlation between height of ceiling and preferred distance.

126

Variations

A replication of Long's (1984) study could be carried out: as experimenters, select areas within the college that are likely to be tense areas, eg outside the principal's office, and relaxed areas, eg common room and give subjects the prepared questionnaire (see opposite).

Analysis

Correlation between ratings of tenseness and average distance indicated on diagram.

Test of difference between situations rated as tense and relaxed.

NB Schacter (1959) found that there was a difference between first-borns and later-borns in their 'need for affiliation' in a stressful, anxiety-provoking situation. He found that more first-borns would choose to wait with others than later-borns. Does this difference interact with Long's (1984) finding? Is there an effect of birth order on interpersonal distance preference in stressful situations?

Questionnaire for interpersonal distance preference

Please could you fill out all the details on this sheet:

AGE:_____   SEX: FEMALE_____
                                  MALE_____

Indicate on the scale below how tense or relaxed you feel at the moment.

Very   Very
Tense   Relaxed

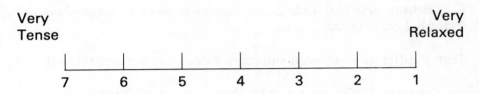

7	6	5	4	3	2	1

In the diagram below the circle is meant to represent you and the solid lines are in front of you and to your sides. Please indicate on each solid line the closest point at which you feel a stranger could stand and leave you still at the same level of relaxation.

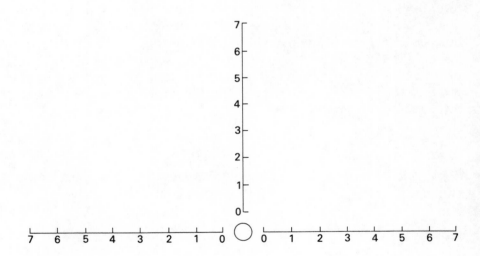

8 Touching and competition

Argyle (1984) reports that there are strict rules regarding bodily contact in our culture, ie who touches who, and when and where these touches take place. He suggests that contact occurs in many rituals to indicate a change of relationship. For example if you touch during a greeting this symbolises that you are more intimate with that person.

Writers who take an ethological perspective (eg Morris, 1978) have suggested that after winning a competition the victors indulge in a triumph display in which they assert their dominance by trying to increase their height, eg jumping in the air, or holding their hands in the air. Can touch also be used as a sign of dominance?

Anderton and Heckel (1984) observed contestants in a swimming competition and found that winners were more likely to initiate touch contacts with other contestants than were losers.

Heckel, Allen and Blackmon (1986) investigated the touching behaviour of winning and losing teams in 100 flag football matches. Both teams were observed immediately following the conclusion of the game by two observers. In all of the categories of touching observed (handshakes and pats on the head, shoulder, stomach, buttock, and back), winners initiated more touches of losers than losers did of winners. The researchers also noted, but did not properly investigate, that losers tended to congregate in small groups, not touching each other, whereas winners tended to touch other team members.

Keywords

Sport; triumph displays; touching behaviour; bodily contact; body contact.

Bibliography

Argyle M (1984) *The Psychology of Interpersonal Behaviour* (4th ed.) Penguin, Harmondsworth.

Heckel, RV, Allen SS and Blackmon DC (1986) 'Tactile Communication of Winners in Flag Football'. *Perceptual and Motor Skills*, 63, 553–554.

Morris, D (1978) *Manwatching*. Triad/Panther, St Albans.

Observations of sports events: darts, athletics, swimming etc. Sports days may be a useful opportunity, or observation in the games room of a public house. Record how many times winners and losers initiate touch, following the conclusion of the contest.

Analysis

Graphical/chi-squared goodness of fit.

---

9 The postdecision dissonance effect

Background

Festinger's (1957) Theory of cognitive dissonance has the central assumption that people are motivated to avoid dissonance and achieve consonance.

Dissonance is the unpleasant experience that a person has when they are aware that there is inconsistency between either their behaviour and their thoughts, or between two or more thoughts. Classic examples of dissonance include: the person who smokes and yet values their health, or the person who likes eating lots of chocolates but wants to lose weight. These people will, according to the theory, experience dissonance and will be motivated to either change their behaviour or their thoughts. The person who likes eating a lot of chocolate can therefore either stop eating chocolate (change of behaviour), or change their thoughts regarding their weight. (For a fuller description of the theory see Aronson, 1980).

The theory predicts that after having made a decision, a person will view that decision as the best decision possible. This enables them to avoid the dissonance that would be experienced if they thought 'I chose this when the other choices would have been better'. In effect, the theory says that people justify their decisions by increasing the value of the alternative that they chose.

(NB Once a person has chosen a particular alternative their behaviour cannot be changed; their only option, to avoid dissonance, is to change their thoughts about their behaviour.)

This postdecision dissonance is particularly likely to occur when:

- there are several attractive alternatives;
- there are no real criteria for deciding between the alternatives;
- there is no way of changing the decision once it has been made.

One situation that fits this description is gambling. Knox and Inkster (1968) reported that racetrack betters expressed more confidence in their bets when asked after they had placed them, than when asked immediately before they had placed them. Younger, Walker and Arrowood (1977) found that subjects had greater confidence that they would win at Bingo if they were asked after they had paid than if they were asked prior to paying.

Tedeschit (1981) argued that these findings could be explained without using Cognitive Dissonance theory, and explained the effect in terms of 'impression management'. The predecision groups could be expressing more moderate, or less confident, attitudes about their impending decision for reasons of modesty or embarrassment.

There are thus two alternative explanations for the difference between pre- and post-decision groups. The cognitive dissonance explanation suggests that members of the post-decision group increase their confidence to avoid dissonance. The impression management explanation suggests that the pre-decision group decrease their confidence ratings to avoid negative impressions. Rosenfeld, Kennedy and Giacalone (1986) pointed out that the two studies mentioned above did not use a control group of people who did not make a decision. They suggested that a control group would help decide between the two alternative explanations. They carried out a study in a shopping arcade where there was a 'gumball guess' lottery being held (i.e How many sweets are there in a jar?). They asked people to rate their chance of winning on a scale of 1–100. The subjects included a pre-decision group, a post-decision group, and a no-decision control group. The results showed no difference between the pre-decision group and the control group, but the post-decision group had significantly greater confidence than both of the other groups.

The results appeared to be more consistent with the cognitive dissonance explanation, but the researchers suggested that this did not exclude impression management explanations altogether. It could be that the post-decision enhancement could be interpreted as face saving.

Keywords

Cognitive dissonance; post-choice dissonance; post-decision dissonance; impression management

Bibliography

Rosenfeld R, Kennedy JG, Giacalone RA (1986) 'Decision making: A demonstration of the Postdecision Dissonance Effect'. *The Journal of Social Psychology*, 126, 663–665.
Aronson E (1980) *The Social Animal* (3rd ed.) WH Freeman and Co., San Francisco.

Possible methods

Many field studies are possible, including replications of the studies above.

Find or create a situation that fulfills the criteria for post-choice dissonance to occur (see above). Fairs or fetes may be suitable opportunities. Charity events often encourage people to gamble for a good cause. Or anybody that is selling raffle tickets could collect the data.

Ask subjects to rate chances of winning: some before they make their choice (pre-decision group), some after they have made their choice (post-decision group). (The subjects can be asked to rate their chances on a scale.)

Analysis

Graphical/test(s) of difference.

If Rosenfeld *et al*'s study is replicated it may be advisable to have separate hypotheses relating to: control group v pre-decision group; control group v post-decision group; pre-decision v post-decision group.

10 False consensus, personal experience and the availability heuristic

Background

We often hear people using such phrases as: 'Most normal people feel . . .' or 'The majority of people think that . . .'. These phrases are often said with confidence and conviction, even if the person could not possibly know what the majority of people think or feel. It could be that these phrases are just ways of speaking, or it could be that people use them to add weight to what they think or feel. Some psychologists now maintain, on the basis of research, that in many cases when a person uses such phrases they are reflecting their own true beliefs.

Ross, Greene and House (1977) coined the term 'The False Consensus Effect' (FCE) to refer to the tendency for people to regard their own behaviour, judgements and characteristics as relatively typical within the overall population. The researchers asked students whether they would walk around their college for half an hour wearing a sandwich board advertising a restaurant. Those students that agreed estimated that two-thirds of the college would do the same. Those that refused estimated that two-thirds would refuse.

Sherman *et al* (1983) found that teenage smokers were more likely to overestimate the number of smokers.

Fields and Schuman (1976), in surveys in Detroit, found that often when a person held a political view that was found to be in the minority in that area, they estimated that the majority of people would hold that view.

Most explanations for the FCE suggest that it occurs because of self-serving motivational biases. That is, it serves our own purposes and goals to believe that our behaviour and judgements are normal within the overall population. Sherman *et al* (1983), for example, suggested that the need for social support may be the cause of a person wanting to believe that what they do is normal.

Bennet and Hibbard (1986) suggest that the motivational account of the FCE has been too readily accepted by psychologists. They note that, until their study, all research into the FCE had been concerned with voluntary behaviour and judgements. They suggest that self-serving motivational biases cannot account for the effect if it occurs regardless of personal goals, judgements or beliefs. To investigate this possibility they looked at people who had been the victim of a crime – something over which a person does not have voluntary control.

They surveyed 190 people and found that 27% of the sample had been a victim in the last 12 months of at least one of the 17 categories of crime that they asked about. (The crimes included rape, burglary, threatening behaviour, car theft, assault and vandalism.) The researchers then compared victims and non-victims on their responses to the question: 'How much crime in general do you think there is in this area?'. The results were highly significant, with victims estimating a much higher crime rate in the area than non-victims.

Bennet and Hibbard (1986) believe that self-motivational biases cannot account for this finding; they suggest an explanation with reference to the 'availability heuristic' (Tversky and Khaneman, 1973). Heuristics are guiding principles in our thought processes that allow us to make judgements in complex situations. The availability heuristic refers to the finding that a person's estimate of the frequency of events is strongly influenced by the availability of relevant cases of that event in memory. Thus Bennet and Hibbard (1986) suggest that victims of crime have a relevant memory of their experience and due to this have higher estimates of crime than non-victims who do not have a relevant memory.

Keywords

Attribution; false consensus effect; self-serving biases; perception of crime.

Bibliography

Bennet M and Hibbard M (1986) 'Availability and the False Consensus Effect'. *The Journal of Social Psychology*, 126, 403–405.
Sears DO, Peplau LA, Freedman JL, and Taylor SE (1988) *Social Psychology* (4th ed.) Prentice Hall, London.

Possible methods

A survey which partially replicated Bennet and Hibbard's study could be carried out:

Prepare survey questionnaire to include:

a) a question about whether people have been a victim of certain categories of crime (as above or by contacting the local police for a list of the most commonly reported crimes);

b) a question about incidence of crime in the area followed by a five-point scale (a great deal, quite a lot, not a lot, very little, don't know).

Analysis

Graphical/complex chi-squared test comparing victims and non-victims.

Variations

- If people know of others who have been victims but have not been victims themselves, does this affect their estimate? Compare groups: know a victim vs do not know a victim.

- Other topics might include: incidence of smoking estimates between smokers and non-smokers; incidence of drug use and estimates of drug use; support for political parties and estimates of support in people under 18. Is there a relationship between the number of friends a person has and their estimate of the average number of friends people have?

NB A person cannot choose their own first name. Is there a relationship between the number of other students a student knows with the same name as them and their estimate of the number of people with that name in the school/college. Access to school/college registers could find actual incidence if accuracy of judgement was of interest.

---

11 Belief in horoscopes

Background

Tyson (1982) reports that reviews of the research on astrology indicate that there is little empirical support for astrological theory. Despite these findings many people still believe in horoscopes, and many more regularly read their horoscopes.

135

Belief in horoscopes that describe a person's personality can be explained with reference to three major factors:

a) generality

b) specificity

c) favourability.

Generality

Horoscopes usually provide very general statements about a person's personality. Snyder and Shenkel (1975) found that people will readily accept the accuracy of generalised personality descriptions. O'Dell (1972) even found that some subjects would perceive a generalised personality description as more accurate than a personality profile gained from a psychometric test.

Meehl (1956) called the acceptance of generalised personality descriptions the 'Barnum effect', after PT Barnum whose circus' success was thought to be based on the notion that there should be 'a little something for everybody' (Snyder *et al*, 1977).

Specificity

This refers to how specific or 'individual' a person perceives the description to be. If the subject is told that the description covers most people in general (low specificity) they will have less faith in it than in one that has been drawn up specially for them (high specificity). Snyder (1974) demonstrated that this was true for horoscopes. He found that subjects who were told that their horoscope was based on the year, month and date of birth would judge it as being more accurate than subjects who were told that the horoscope was based on only the year and the month of birth. (In fact the same descriptions were given to both groups.) The more specific the time referent was, the more accurate the horoscope was perceived to be.

Favourability

A number of studies have demonstrated that the more favourable a personality description is, the more likely a subject is to accept that description as accurate (Tyson, 1982).

As well as the above three factors, research has suggested that personality and social factors may characterise people who believe in horoscopes. Tyson (1979) found that people who consult astrologers are likely to be experiencing poor social relationships.

Snyder (1972) found that people with an external locus of control were more likely to accept generalised personality descriptions, and Tyson (1979) found that people who read astrology books also tend to have an external locus of control. However, the relationships between locus of control and belief in, or reading of, horoscopes is by no means clear. Sosis et al (1980) and Fichten and Sunerton (1983) found no relationship between locus of control and belief in astrology.

Fichten and Sunerton (1983) found that horoscope reading was related closely to neuroticism on the EPI (Eysenck Personality Inventory). They also found a 'sex' difference in horoscope reading habits, with females tending to read them more often. They explain this difference in terms of the publishing practice of magazines and newspapers, noting that horoscopes are more likely to appear in women's magazines than men's magazines, and in the women's sections of newspapers. They do not conclude whether the publishing policy or the female interest in horoscopes came first.

Belief in horoscopes as personality descriptions may be explainable with reference to the three factors of generality, specificity, and favourability in combination with predisposing personality and social factors.

If a person consults an astrologer, the person is likely to have faith in astrology before they consult them and therefore be pre-disposed to accept the horoscope. Also, astrologers tend to give fairly lengthy descriptions (often a few pages long), which gives scope for generality; they are based on specific information gained from an interview beforehand; and the descriptions tend to be moderately favourable (Tyson, 1979). Thus the conditions are right for the person to accept the accuracy of the description.

Readers of astrology books who find some degree of truth in the general description given of their zodiac sign may conclude that if this general description can be accurate, the description must be really accurate when all the birth information is used. The person is thus starting to convince themselves of the validity of the horoscope before their individual one is case (Tyson, 1982).

137

According to Fichten and Sunerton (1983) very little research has been done on the reliability and validity of horoscope predictions. They compared daily and monthly predictions prepared by different astrologers in different publications and found little reliability in the predictions (ie the predictions were different). To investigate the validity of the predictions they presented subjects with their own and others' horoscope prediction for the previous day, or the previous month, and asked the subjects to rate whether the predictions would have been useful to them if they had read them beforehand. If the predictions were unlabelled, without reference to the zodiac signs, the subjects rated them as not being useful, but when the predictions were labelled the subjects rated their 'own' prediction as being more accurate. Thus a horoscope prediction is perceived as more valid when a person can identify it with their own star sign (high specificity) than when they cannot (low specificity).

Keywords

Horoscope; beliefs; attitudes; astrology; specificity; generality; favourability; validity; reliability; locus of control

Bibliography

Fichten CS and Sunerton B (1983) 'Popular Horoscopes and the "Barnum Effect"', *The Journal of Psychology*, 114, 123–124.
Tyson GT (1982) 'Why people perceive horoscopes as being true: A review', *Bulletin of the British Psychological Society*, 35, 186–188.

Possible methods

A partial replication of Snyder (1974) could be carried out by: obtaining some Zodiac personality descriptions from a magazine or a popular book on Zodiac signs or Sun signs. These could then be used for an independent groups design in which Group A is asked year of birth and month and then given appropriate description. Group B is asked year of birth, month of birth, day and time of birth and given appropriate description.

Both groups are given the same set of descriptions and asked to rate the accuracy of the description on a rating scale: not at all like me . . . to . . . very like me.

Analysis

Graphical/test of difference.

A partial replication of Fichten and Sunerton (1983) investigating the validity of horoscopes could be carried out by: obtaining daily or monthly horoscope predictions; presenting them to subjects after the day/month has gone; and asking the subjects to rate the 12 predictions on a ten-point scale of personal usefulness (How personally useful would this forecast have been for you if you had read it yesterday/last month?).

This again would be an independent groups design: Group A given 12 predictions including zodiac signs; Group B given the same 12 predictions excluding zodiac signs. Both groups would be asked to rate each of the 12 predictions as being useful or not, on a rating scale.

Analysis

Compare each subject's rating of 'own' zodiac sign prediction with average rating for 'other' zodiac signs.

Variations

- Subjects could be presented with either horoscope personality descriptions of monthly/daily horoscope predictions without the zodiac signs, and asked to choose which one is the most accurate description/prediction. (Analysis in terms of expected frequencies/Chi-squared Goodness of fit.)

- A survey could be carried out to determine whether the 'sex' difference observed by Fichter and Sunerton's (1983) American study exists in the UK.

Note that some psychologists regard the deception of subjects for the purpose of experimentation as unethical. It is important to debrief subjects in all experiments but especially important where any deception has taken place. Please consult appropriate ethical guidelines published by the British Psychological Society.

12 Belief in the paranormal

Background

Paranormal phenomena include all the varieties of extra-sensory perception (ESP): mental telepathy (reading someone else's thoughts); clairvoyance (the perception of objects or events not influencing the senses); pre-cognition (perception of a future event); and psycho-kinesis (the ability to move objects or affect machines through the power of thought). The term is sometimes inclusive of supernatural phenomena such as ghosts and poltergeists. Paranormal phenomena are the domain of a branch of psychology known as parapsychology.

Over the years various researchers have claimed to have found evidence for various paranormal phenomena, while others spend their time disproving these claims. For a good short discussion of some of the evidence and some of the difficulties of investigating this area see Atkinson, Atkinson and Hilgard (1981).

Whether paranormal phenomena exist or not, it cannot be denied that a substantial number of people believe in them. Jones *et al* (1977) found that 58% of a sample of students believed in half or more of a list of paranormal phenomena, and 27% claimed to have experienced some paranormal phenomenon. In a random postal survey Blackmore (1984) found that 36% of respondents professed belief in ESP and 44% of these gave their main reason for believing as their own experience.

Blackmore and Troscianko (1985) suggest that if the main reason for belief in the paranormal is experience of these phenomena, this raises the question: 'Why do people believe that they have had paranormal experiences?'

Blackmore and Troscianko suggested that there are two main ways of answering this question. The first is simply to say that these people have had a paranormal experience. The second is that their belief is based upon the misinterpretation of normal events as paranormal. Their investigation looked for a possible basis for the second explanation.

Zusne and Jones (1982) noted that the most commonly reported paranormal phenomena were telepathy and precognitive or prophetic dreams. What these phenomena have in common is that they

140

depend upon judgements of probability. For example, if you dream that the next day you will get a letter from a long-lost friend, and when you wake up you find one, you may be tempted to conclude that the chance of this just being coincidence is too low and therefore you might conclude that your dream prophesied this.

Kahneman and Tversky (1973) showed that reasoning short cuts or heuristics that guide people's thought processes are often biased and may give rise to serious errors in judgements concerning probability.

Blackmore and Troscianko (1985) found evidence which supported the conclusion that believers in paranormal phenomena were less accurate than non-believers in problems involving probability judgement.

Another question regarding belief in the paranormal is why believers will continue to believe in such phenomena even when there is considerable evidence to suggest that they do not exist (Wierzbicki, 1985). An explanation for this might be found in terms of the selective learning hypothesis (Greenwald and Sakamura, 1967). This hypothesis suggests that believers will pay more attention to evidence that confirms their beliefs than to evidence that is not in agreement with their beliefs. Support for the selective learning hypothesis comes from a study by Russell and Jones (1980) in which they found that believers made more errors than sceptics in recalling written abstracts of experiments that contradicted their initial beliefs.

Wierzbicki (1985) suggested that continued belief in the paranormal may be due to the selective learning effect, but he also provides evidence that the degree of belief in paranormal phenomena is significantly correlated with ability to solve reasoning tasks. He found that believers made more errors on a set of reasoning tasks than did sceptics, and suggests that a reason for continued belief in the paranormal may be that believers are unable to use the evidence available to disconfirm their belief.

Keywords

Belief; attitudes; attribution; probability judgements; paranormal; ESP; selective learning

Bibliography

Atkinson RL, Atkinson RC and Hilgard ER (1981) *Introduction to Psychology* (7th ed.) Harcourt Brace Jovanovich, London.

Blackmore S and Torscianko T (1985) 'Belief in the Paranormal: Probability Judgements, illusory control, and the 'chance baseline shift', *The British Journal of Psychology*, 76, 459–468.

Wierzbicki M (1985) 'Reasoning Errors and Belief in the Paranormal', *The Journal of Social Psychology*, 125, 489–494.

Possible methods

A partial replication of Blackmore and Troscianko (1985) could be undertaken. First devise a questionnaire on belief in the paranormal (perhaps using the Likert method, see page 170). Using a repeated measures design, give each subject the questionnaire that you have devised, and a copy of the probability test (page 146).

Your hypothesis could be:

- *correlational* – looking for a relationship between the two sets of scores;

- *experimental* – by dividing the sample into groups on the basis of their questionnaire scores (eg those above the mean counted as believers, and those below sceptics), the groups could be analysed for difference in their scores on the probability test.

Analysis

Compare total score for questionnaire with scores from probability judgements.

Variation

A partial replication of Wierzbicki (1985) could be undertaken, by giving each subject a self-devised questionnaire on belief in the paranormal and the eight reasoning problems on page 144.

The problems are presented in groups of four to allow the order of presentation to be balanced across subjects. Four of the problems are presented in abstract form and four have content relating to paranormal phenomena.

Analysis

Compare the number of problems solved correctly with the scores on the questionnaire. Similarly, hypotheses can either be correlational or experimental.

Alternative study Is there a difference in belief in the paranormal between science students and arts students?

SET 1

Please carefully consider the problems below.

If you think that the last line follows logically from the first two lines, underline VALID. If you do not think that the last line follows logically from the first two lines underline INVALID.

1 If A is true, then B will be observed.
   A is true.
   Therefore B will be observed.

                                                        VALID/INVALID

2 If psycho-kinesis exists then a person can move an object by thought power.
   A person cannot move an object by thought power.
   Therefore psycho-kinesis does not exist.

                                                        VALID/INVALID

3 If A is true then B will be observed.
   A is not true.
   Therefore B will not be observed.

                                                        VALID/INVALID

4 If precognition exists then a person can perceive a future event.
   A person can perceive a future event.
   Therefore precognition exists.

                                                        VALID/INVALID

SET 2

Please consider the problems below carefully.

If you think that the last line follows logically from the first two lines underline VALID. If you do not think that the last line follows logically from the first two lines underline INVALID.

1 If clairvoyance exists then a person can perceive a hidden object.
  Clairvoyance does not exist.
  Therefore a person cannot perceive a hidden object.

  VALID/INVALID

2 If A is true then B will be observed.
  B is observed.
  Therefore A is true.

  VALID/INVALID

3 If mental telepathy exists then a person can read another person's thoughts.
  Mental telepathy exists.
  Therefore a person can read another person's thoughts.

  VALID/INVALID

4 If A is true then B will be observed.
  B is not observed.
  Therefore A is not true.

  VALID/INVALID

Questionnaire on Probability

1 A bag contains 10 red and 10 blue counters. I pull out 10 counters and 8 of them are red. Am I more likely to get red or blue next time?

RED ☐
BLUE ☐
EITHER EQUALLY LIKELY ☐

2 A bag contains buttons that are either green or yellow, in unknown proportion. Of 10 buttons taken out, 8 were yellow. Which is more likely to be pulled out next?

GREEN ☐
YELLOW ☐
EITHER EQUALLY LIKELY ☐

3 A coin is tossed to decide whether Bill or Doris does the washing up. Doris has done the washing up for the last four evenings. Who is more likely to do the washing up this evening?

BILL ☐
DORIS ☐
EITHER EQUALLY LIKELY ☐

4 How many people would you need to have in a group to have a 50:50 chance that two of them have the same Birthday (not counting year)?

22 ☐
43 ☐
96 ☐

Adapted from Blackmore, S and Troscianko, T (1985).

13 Lateral cradling preferences in males and females

Background

Salk (1973) suggested that an infant became 'imprinted' upon the sound of its mother's heartbeat; after birth, if the infant was held with its head to the left rather than the right it would be calmed by the sound of the heart. Salk observed that there was a preference for women to hold infants in their left arm with the head towards the left when cradling newborns. Since Salk's original suggestion many studies have confirmed this finding, using a variety of methods: Dagenbach, Harris and Fitzgerald (1985) used direct observations of parents and infants; Bundy (1979) observed the cradling of a doll by college students; Harris and Fitzgerald (1985) analysed photographs in undergraduate textbooks of developmental psychology, and also reported in the same paper that the preference occurs in the absence of a baby or a doll if students are asked to close their eyes and imagine cradling a three-month-old baby.

All these studies have found a preference for left side cradling. The results have ranged from approximately 60 to 80% with the majority of studies being in the 65 to 75% range.

The pattern for cradling preferences for men has not been so clear, with some studies showing a weak preference for the left, some showing no preference for either side, and some studies showing a preference for the right side. The exceptions are the studies that have found an equal left side cradling preference for males (Bundy, 1969; Harris and Fitzgerald, 1985).

Why women show a left-sided preference whereas men, on the whole, do not, is unclear. Rheingold and Keene (1965) found no lateral holding preferences for inanimate objects, such as bags of groceries, in men or women. Left- and right-handed women show the same degree of left-side cradling, and with 88–90% of the population being right-handed (Porac and Coren, 1981) it seems that there is no simple relationship between lateral cradling preferences and handedness.

Proposed explanations for the sex difference (if one exists) are varied. Salk (1973) suggested it was because of the calming effect of the mother's heartbeat. Rheingold and Keene (1965) suggest that when men carry children the child is often older and heavier, and therefore there is a shift towards the usually stronger right side.

147

Bundy (1979) suggested that this might be an explanation for the absence of the sex difference in his study, as he used a small doll. These findings are also consistent with those of Dagenbach *et al* (1985), in which the left-sided preference diminished for both males and females the older the infant was.

Keywords

Laterality; lateral preferences; handedness; foetal imprinting; sex differences; cradling.

Bibliography

Harris LJ and Fitzgerald HE (1985) 'Lateral Cradling preferences in Men and Women: Results from a Photographic Study', *Journal of General Psychology*, 112(2), 185–189.

Possible methods

Variations on this study could include:

Photographic study Rate photographs of adults cradling infants in books/magazines as male/female, left side/right side (excluding pictures of breast feeding).

Doll study Ask males/females to cradle a doll. This could be extended to two dolls, one light and one heavy to test Bundy's (1979) hypothesis.

Direct observation Studies could take place in a mother and baby clinic, or of children playing with dolls. When does 'sex' difference begin? Is this due to nature or nurture?

Role playing Ask subjects to close their eyes and imagine they are holding a) a small baby; b) a two-year-old child. Do 'sex differences' occur in role-played situations? (If there is a drama course in your school or college it may be possible to arrange for the drama students to role-play situations.)

Inanimate objects In contrast to the findings of Rheingold and Keene (1965) students of mine have found a sex difference in shopping bag carrying through observational studies in town centres. NB It would be possible to compare lateral preference for inanimate objects and infants in the same subjects, if you asked them to role play a number of different scenes.

148

For all the studies above it is recommended that large samples are used.

Analysis

All above studies will provide frequency data. Chi-squared goodness of fit.

---

14 Preference for sex of child

Background

The sex of a child is, realistically, out of the control of a mother or father and yet many will express a preference for one sex. Studies in the USA, Great Britain and the Netherlands have confirmed the popular belief that the overall preference is for males (Williamson, 1977). Parke (1981), also reports that this preference is present in India and Brazil, as well as a number of other countries.

Freudian theory would explain women wishing for a baby boy in terms of unresolved electra-conflicts and penis envy. Horney (1939) pointed out that Freud's theory involves the assumption that the male body is perfect and that the female body incomplete and imperfect. Many people dismiss the Freudian interpretation on the grounds of sexism.

The large majority of the studies have been questionnaire studies of college students, or married couples in fertility studies. Invariably they found a preference for males, with very little difference in the degree of preference expressed by males and females.

It has also been found that the sex preference for laterborns can be affected by the sex of the first born (Steinbacher and Gilroy, 1985). Lois Hoffman (1977) conducted an extensive survey of 1500 women and 400 men, and found couples are more likely to have other children if they only have girls. They will even continue to have more children than they had planned, if they are trying for a boy.

Steinbacher and Gilroy (1985) suggest that asking hypothetical questions of subjects who have not been through pregnancy, or are not pregnant, may lead to less accurate results than if women who are pregnant for the first time (primiparous women) are asked. Research on attitude and behaviour consistency has found that the

149

more salient and relevant an attitude is, the more consistent it is with behaviour. As the attitude to the sex of their offspring is more relevant to primiparous women their preference should be more consistent with their true choice.

Studies of primiparous women have provided mixed results:

	Male preference	Female preference	No preference
Uddenberg *et al* (1971)	46%	32%	22%
Oakley (1978)	54%	22%	25%
Steinbacher and Gilroy (1985)	15%	26%	59%

Steinbacher and Gilroy's (1985) study differs from the other two in that the sex difference is reversed, and there is a greater proportion of women who express no preference. They also found a slight trend for women who were strong supporters of the women's movement to prefer girls. They suggest that their results are explainable in terms of a gradual weakening of the societal bias against women.

Parke (1981) reports that among men the preference for a male child is particularly strong, with between three and four times as many men preferring boys as compared to girls. Are male preferences for sex of child changing as well?

Keywords

Preference for child; preference for sex of child; sex bias of parents; primiparous women; penis envy; Freudian theory.

Bibliography

Parke RD (1981) *Fathering*, Fontana, Glasgow.
Hall C and Lindzey G (1978) *Theories of Personality*, (3rd ed.) John Wiley and Sons, USA.
Steinbacher R and Gilroy FD (1985) 'Preference for Sex of child among Primiparous Women', *The Journal of Psychology*, 119, 541–547.

Possible methods

Data could be collected in the following ways:

- A survey of male and female college students or members of the public, asking them about their preferences were they to have a child. If possible, access to a prenatal clinic waiting room to ask expectant mothers/fathers about their preferences would allow a more accurate confirmation of Steinbacher and Gilroy's study.

- A survey asking parents whether they enjoy male or female children more.

- A survey asking children of different ages whether they would want a boy or a girl if they had children when they were grown up. This would shed light on when preferences start to emerge.

- A survey of students asking for ideal composition of a family. This would find out whether the preference occurs when subjects are not forced into a preference.

Analysis

All the above studies would provide frequency data. The data could first be analysed in terms of percentages, and chi-squared goodness of fit test could be applied.

---

15 Preference for surnames

Background

Zajonc's Exposure Hypothesis (1968) suggests that increased exposure to a stimulus will lead to an increased liking for that stimulus. Zajonc is therefore proposing a monotonic linear relationship (Figure 15a).
NB Monotonic means that the relationship only goes in one direction. In this example the direction is positive, ie it increases from left to right.

Other researchers (eg Sluckin, 1980) have found an inverted 'U' relationship in research into the relationship between familiarity and preference (Figure 15b).

The difference between investigations that find a monotonic linear relationship and those that find an inverted U relationship may be in the type of stimuli they have used. Colman, Sluckin and Hargreaves (1981), suggest there are two classes of stimuli that will provide the two different relationships:

151

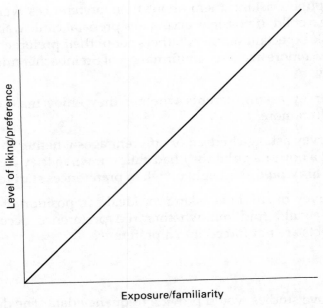

Fig 15a

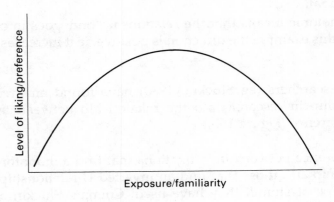

Fig 15b

Class A stimuli – where a person has voluntary control over how many times they are exposed to them.

Class B stimuli – where a person has little or no voluntary control over how often they are exposed to them.

Colman *et al* (1981) suggest that an inverted U relationship underlies both class A and B stimuli, but because of what they call the preference-feedback hypothesis, Class A stimuli will only display a monotonic linear relationship.

They reason that Class A stimuli will only be voluntarily chosen by people while increased exposure still leads to increased liking. As soon as increased exposure starts to lead to a decrease in liking, the person will choose not to expose themselves to the stimuli. An everyday example of Class A stimuli is a popular record. Once you have bought it, you play it regularly until you feel that you have heard it too much; then you stop playing it. You might then find that after a time you start playing it again, and you may go through phases of playing it or not playing it.

Colman *et al* (1981) suggest that first names or Christian names go through cycles of being fashionable because of this preference feedback effect. As soon as a name becomes too familiar, parents stop choosing that name. In support of this hypothesis they found a monotonic linear relationship between familiarity of Christian names and the degree of preference for these names.

Class B stimuli cannot be affected by the preference-feedback effect, because, by definition, people have no control over their exposure.

Colman *et al* (1981) suggested that surnames were a good example of Class B stimuli, and their investigation found evidence for an inverted U relationship.

Keywords

Preference; attitudes; familiarity; exposure

Bibliography

Colman M, Sluckin W, and Hargreaves DJ (1981) 'The effect of familiarity on preference for surnames', *British Journal of Psychology*, 72, 363–369.

Possible methods

Adapting the method used by Colman *et al* (1981) the following study could be undertaken on surnames:

1 Randomly select 30 surnames from a local telephone directory (avoiding double-barrelled names) and list them on a copy of the prepared questionnaire (see page 155).

2 Use an independent groups design (this is recommended by Colman *et al* – or a repeated measures could be used if not enough subjects are available):

Condition A: Give subjects a copy of the questionnaire on page 156, ask them to rate the surnames for familiarity on the rating scale.

Condition B: Give subjects a copy of the questionnaire on page 155; ask them to rate the names for liking/preference.

(NB In selecting the names for study, ensure that the sample includes some names that are very common and some that are rare. Sex of subjects may be a potential independent variable, due to females adopting different surnames on marriage.)

Analysis

Work out mean familiarity rating and mean preference rating for each surname, and plot on scattergram.

Further analysis: Either divide the range of familiarity into thirds; or find ten least familiar and ten most familiar.

Whichever of the above methods is chosen the aim is to compare the lowest third with the highest third. If there is an inverted U relationship there should be a positive correlation for the lowest third, and a negative correlation for the highest third.

Variations

What is the relationship for word frequency? See lists of words differing in frequency (page 159). Are words Class A or Class B stimuli?

Questionnaire on preference for names

For each name listed below, fill in the rating scale indicating how much you personally like or dislike the name.

Name	Dislike 0	1	2	3	Like 4

AGE: SEX:

Questionnaire on familiarity of names

For each name listed below fill in the rating scale indicating how common or rare you think these names are in this area.

Name	Very rare 0	1	2	3	Very common 4

AGE: SEX:

Appendices

Appendix A Word lists

The word lists that appear on the following pages are all four letter common nouns. The lists vary in frequency of occurrence according to the 'Thorndike-Lorge word count'. (The Thorndike-Lorge word count was a very lengthy study that examined printed material and recorded how frequently words were used.)

List A: Words in the first five hundred most frequent words (0–500)

List B: Words in the second five hundred most frequent words (501–1000)

List C: Words that occur between 30 and 50 times per million

List D: Words that occur less than 10 times per million

List E: Words that occur less than 20 times per four million

The words can be photocopied and enlarged, cut out and stuck on to cards for manual presentation. Or if your college has a memory drum or tachistoscope they can be used with these machines.

Investigations using the lists

Apart from the investigations detailed in other parts of this book, a number of well-quoted effects can be demonstrated with words of differing frequency:

1 High-frequency words are recognised as words quicker than low-frequency words.

A tachistoscope would be needed to give a formal demonstra-

tion of this, comparing reaction times to high and low frequency words, in a decision task that asks the subject to decide
between words and non-words. The effect may be seen in
solution times to word squares containing words of different
frequencies. Word squares with higher frequency words should
be completely solved (ie all the words found) more quickly then
squares with lower frequency words. Similarly, if a fixed period
of time is used more high frequency words should be recognised. (Word square 1 on page 164 uses the words from List B;
Word Square 2 on page 165 uses the words from List D.)

2 Anagrams of high-frequency words are solved quicker than
   anagrams of low-frequency words. The effect would be very
   small with these short words but should be detectable. (See
   Gardiner, 1975, for a similar experiment.)

3 High-frequency words are remembered more easily than low-
   frequency words. This could easily be demonstrated in a
   repeated measures design using two lists of differing frequency.

Paivio (1972) has provided convincing evidence that imageability of
words is more important than frequency. Following Paivio's line of
research it would be possible to subject all or some of the lists to the
following tests:

One group rates the words for ease of imageability from *Very easy to
provide an image* to *Difficult to create an image*. Another group is given
lists of words to remember.

The results would show which words were forgotten the most
frequently across the group, and by using correlational analysis it
could be worked out whether word frequency or imageability was
the most predictive.

References

Gardiner JM and Kaminska Z (1975) *First Experiments in Psychology*
Methuen, London.
Thorndike EL and Lorge I (1944) *The teacher's word book of 30,000
words*. Teacher's College Press, New York.

LIST A

BALL
BANK
BEAR
BIRD
CASE
FACE
FIRE
FOOT
FOOD
GOLD
HAIR
HAND
LAND
LINE
MILK
ROAD
ROCK
SAIL
STEP
WORD

LIST B

BABY
BAND
BELL
BOAT
BONE
CAKE
COAL
COAT
GATE
HALL
IRON
LAKE
PAGE
PATH
SALT
SAND
SEAT
SHOE
TAIL
WING

LIST C

ARCH
BARN
BATH
BEAR
BELT
BULL
CAGE
CORD
DART
DRUM
FORT
LAMB
LANE
PEER
POOL
RICE
SHED
SOAP
VEIN
WEED

LIST D

ATOM

BERG

CHEF

CLAM

CLOT

DICE

DENT

FANG

FLEA

HALO

HOSE

KILT

RAFT

RAMP

SOOT

STAG

TALC

TAPE

TART

WEIR

LIST E

APSE
BUNG
BYRE
CHIT
DACE
DILL
FLOE
GAUD
GOBY
IBEX
JAMB
KELP
POCK
RUNE
SAGO
SHIM
TONG
ULNA
VOLE
YAWL

Word square 1

Please look for the hidden four-letter words in the square. Words can be horizontal from left to right, but not right to left or: vertical top to bottom, but not bottom to top. Words cannot be diagonal.

```
G O P D X L F E N C Q S U Y T R A F Z J I L M O C
Z F A N O J D M L I V T I G R L C H O Q E C J P A
E N C B A B Y Q S U I J R A Y K I B L G A T E F T
D P I M L E R T Y D H X O T F A U Q K O S J N Z Y
M Q T N L S Y C I V T A N C P N F E B X P U I D E
F I G N U L R Q O H C L K J S Z E A R T D L H I N
U L A K E J O S H O E N A F K Y E D O R X I A G P
V C I A L T H P T Q A A L P C I U Y X B S E L R J
D E Y K X B E N G I B N S E C T B E L L T H L A M
I Q C B A O J M E P D H T C E A B F E Y B E S L U
E V A E T A C E P F K J T A G Y L L S A O X P M N
X I T E D T Z J D T A C O A L X S E A B E N C J T
P H Y U J H O I E P F K S Y Z E A P L H P E F O R
D T E A Z Q O H V D U I C O B I Y S T L N U L A N
L C N D N R K T U M J P N E A Y T A C W P F Z D I
H E P Y C O A T G R O M A C N F U E N B E A S K G
T A J S N A L A W D T A X R D L Q J O A S N E E F
L B M K E T D A I J T Q L H L D P X E I D X A V T
Q F I J N M P X Z O A S Y G A T J O L A A M T I D
J E G F L E O Y S P I O T A E V G K C A K E M E S
I Y T P P A T H E W L A K P O A C E I V T U S R P
A S V E N H J U N I N D O A B R N T A L X C Y N B
D A H I H B O N E A X A S G C O N F A C G W I N G
T N C O T Y E N P C N H E E M V W I I S K J T L E
E D A H O R K E N S I L D P F E I Y F L D A E W R
```

Word square 2

Please look for the hidden four-letter words in the square. Words can be horizontal from left to right, but not right to left or: vertical top to bottom, but not bottom to top. Words cannot be diagonal.

```
R W E A D L F Y I E F P D L I S N E K O R H A T E
E L T J K S I I W V M T E H N C P N E Y T O C A T
T A R T G C A F N O C A S A X W S T A G H I H L D
B N Y C X L A T N R B P O D N I N U J H N E Y C A
P R S U T V I E C A O E K A R F E S O O T P T Y I
S E M W E I R K G V E A T O A P S Y O E L F G E J
D I R M A A L O J T A G Y S M O Z X P M N J I F Q
T V A X D I E X P D L H L Q P J I A D T E K M B L
F E F N S A O J Q L H R X A T D N A W A N S J A T
G K T A E B N E U F O C A M O R G H A L O Y P E H
I D Z F P O C A T Y S E N P J M U T K R N D N C L
N A W U N G K S Y I E O C I U D V H O Q Z A E T D
R O F E P H I P A E Z Y S K F P E I O H T U V H P
T J C N E B L E S X F L E A A T D J Z C D E T I X
N M P X O A T L L Y G A T J K F P E C L T E A V E
U L S E B Y E F B A E C T H O P E M J A A B C Q I
M A F H T D E N T T C E S N B I G N E M X K Y E D
J R A E S B X Y U I C P L A A Q T P H T L A I C V
P G N I X R O D W Y K F A N D I C E O J C H E F U
N I G L O T R A E Z S J K L C H O Q R L N U G I F
E D I U P X B E F N P C B A T V I C Y S L N T Q M
Y Z N J S O K Q W A F T E X H D Y T R E L M I P D
T F C L O T L B I K Y A R J U I S Q A T O M C N E
A P J C E Q O H C L R G G T V I L M D J O N A F Z
C O M L I J Z F A W T Y U S Q C N E F L X D P O G
```

Solution to word square 1

```
g o p d x l f e n c q s u y t r a f z j i l m o c
z f a n o j d m l i v t I g r l c h o q e c j p a
e n c B A B Y q s u i j I R O a y k i b l I G A T E f t
d p i m l e r t y d h x O t f a u q k o s j n z y
m q t n l s y c i v t a N c p n f e b x p u i d e
f i g n u l r q o h c l k j s z e a r t d l H i n
u L A K E j o S H O E n a f k y e d o r x i A l r j
v c i a l t h p t q a a l p c i u y x b s e L a m
d e y k x B e n g i b n s e c t B E L L t h L a m
i q c b a O j m e p d h t c e a b f e y b e s l u
e v a e t A c e p f k j t a g y l l S a o x p m n
x i t e d T z j d t a C O A L x s e A b e n c j t
p h y u j h o i e p f k s y z e a p L h p e f o r
d t e a z q o h v d u i c o B i y s T l n u l a n
l c n d n r k t u m j p n e A y t a c w p f z d i
h e p y C O A T g r o m a c N f u e n b e a S k g
t a j s n a l a w d t a x r D l q j o a s n E e f
l b m k e t d a i j T q l h l d p x e i d x A i d
q f i j n m p x z o A s y g a t j o l a a m T i d
j e g f l e o y s p I o t a e v g k C A K E m e s
i y t p P A T H e w L a k P o a c e i v t u s r p
a S v e n h j u n i n d o A b R n t a l x c y n b
d A h i h B O N E a x a s G c O n f a c g W I N G
t N c o t y e n p c n h e E m V w i i s k j t l e
e D a h o r k e n s i l d p f E i y f l d a e w r
```

Solution to word square 2

```
r w e a d l f y i e f p d l i s n e k o r H A T E
e l t j k s i i w v m T e h n c p n e y t o c A t
T A R T g c a f n o c A s a x w S T A G h i h L d
b n y c x l a t n r b P o d n i n u j h n e y C a
p r s u t v i e c a o E k a R f e S O O T p t y i
s e m W E I R k g v e a t o A p s y o e l f g e j
d i R m a a l o j t a g y s M o z x p m n j i f q
t v A x d i e x p d l h l q P j i a d t e k m b l
g k T a e b n e u f O c a m o r g H A L O y p e h
i d z f p o c a t y S e n p j m u t k r n d n c l
n a w u n g K s y i E o c i u d v h o q z a e t d
r o f e p h I p a e z y s k f p e i o h t u v h p
t j c n e b L e s x F L E A a t d j z C d e t i x
n m p x o a T l l y g A t j k f p e c L t e a v e
u l s e b y e f b a e C t h o p e m j A a b c q i
m a F h t D E N T t c E s n b i g n e M x k y e d
j r A e s b x y u i c p l a a q t p h t l a i c v
p g N i x r o d w y k f a n D I C E o j C H E F u
n i G l o t r a e z s j k l c h o q r l n u g i f
e d i u p x b e f n p c B a t v i c y s l n t q m
y z n j s o k q w a f t E x h d y t r e l m i p d
t f C L O T l b i k y a R j u i s q A T O M c n e
a p j c e q o h c l r g G t v i l m d j o n a f z
c o m l i j z f a w t y u s q c n e f l x d p o g
```

166

Appendix C Flashcards

Equations for use in distractor task

CORRECT	INCORRECT
$1 + 3 = 4$	$1 + 3 = 5$
$8 - 3 = 5$	$8 - 3 = 6$
$4 \times 3 = 12$	$4 \times 3 = 11$
$4 - 2 = 2$	$4 - 2 = 1$
$6 + 3 = 9$	$6 + 3 = 8$
$1 \times 1 = 1$	$1 \times 1 = 0$
$7 + 4 = 11$	$7 + 4 = 12$
$9 - 5 = 4$	$9 - 5 = 5$
$5 \times 4 = 20$	$5 \times 4 = 18$
$3 - 3 = 0$	$3 - 3 = 1$

Digits to make flashcards

1   2   3   4

5   6   7   8

9   10

Letters to make flashcards

A B C D

E F G H

I J K L

M N O P

Q R S T

U V W X

Y Z

Appendix D Instructions for constructing a questionnaire using the Likert method

1 Decide on the topic of the questionnaire, eg belief in the paranormal; attitudes to nuclear weapons.

2 Generate statements for possible inclusion in the questionnaire. The statements should make one point only. To ensure a wide range, the statements should be generated by a group of individuals and not from just one person.

3 Collate the statements generated in Step 2. Discard repetitions, or any statements that are badly worded and likely to be misunderstood.

4 Present the list of statements to a group of people and ask them to judge individually whether agreement with the statement reflects a positive attitude towards the topic, or a negative attitude – or belief vs disbelief. (NB Ideally this group should be different from the group that generated the statements.)

5 Select the statements on which there is a clear agreement between the raters as to whether the statements are positive or negative.

6 Select an equal number of positive and negative statements from the results of Step 5 and put them into a random order.

7 Put the statements on to a questionnaire and follow each statement with a five-point rating scale ranging from *Strongly agree* to *Strongly disagree*.

Scoring the questionnaire

Once the questionnaire has been completed by the subjects the answer needs to be scored. The five-point scale allows each statement to be given a value from one to five.

If you want the highest scores to go to the subjects that most strongly agree with positive statements, then strongly agreeing with a positive statement should be scored as five and strongly disagreeing scored as one. For negative statements the scores must be reversed so that strongly disagreeing gets a score of five, and strongly agreeing gets a score of one. For example:

	Strongly agree				Strongly disagree
A positive statement	5	4	3	2	1
A negative statement	1	2	3	4	5

If you want the highest scores to go to the subjects that most strongly agree with negative statements the scoring system is reversed, for example:

	Strongly agree				Strongly disagree
A positive statement	5	4	3	2	1
A negative statement	1	2	3	4	5

Whichever method is used, the subjects' final score is found by adding up the scores for each of the statements.

Notes on the construction of Likert scales as a class exercise

The instructions on page 170 can be given to students but they will probably need to be guided through the construction. The instructions will serve the dual purpose of helping the class to construct a questionnaire, and serve as valuable notes of the process for inclusion in their procedure section of a practical reports.

The whole process will probably take about two hours of class time. This can be speeded up if a word processor can be used in the classroom to help collate the statements, which will then need to be printed out and photocopied so that students can vote on whether they are positive or negative statements.

The voting (step 4) is best carried out by a show of hands. It is worth ensuring beforehand that each individual is very clear what they are voting for as I have experienced great confusion with classes during this stage.

If the procedure has been run through once in class, more able students on A level or BTEC national courses may be able to use the instructions on their own in subsequent practicals.

Notes on the use of the checklist page

Whether students are planning their own experiments or being guided through a practical in class, many will fail to obtain the relevant information necessary to either carry out the experiment or write up the report of the experiment. I have found that using a checklist similar to this can help get rid of these problems. It may only be necessary to use the checklist for the first couple of experiments as more able students will then remember what information they need to collect.

Things that should be known before the experiment

1. What is the hypothesis? _____

   _____

2. What is the null hypothesis? _____

   _____

3. Is the hypothesis one-tailed or two-tailed

ONE-TAILED		TWO-TAILED	

4. What is the independent variable? _____

   _____

5. What is the dependent variable? _____

   _____

6. What level of measurement is the data?

NOMINAL		INTERVAL		ORDINAL		RATIO	

7. What type of design is being used?

INDEPENDENT GROUPS	
REPEATED MEASURES	
MATCHED GROUPS	

8. What level of significance will be acceptable? _____

   _____

9. What factors are being kept constant? _____

   _____

10. Things that will need to be found out after the experiment if data is interval or ratio scale

Are the samples of equal variance?

YES		NO	

Are the samples normally distributed?

YES		NO	

Answers

Section 1

Pages 12–13

1 The hypothesis tested: the more expensive the shampoo the more it would tangle my hair; or expensive shampoos contain a tangling agent; or there is a relationship between the cost of the shampoo and the number of times the hair needs to be combed to be tangle free.

2 I tested the hypothesis by: comparing how tangled my hair was after washing it in differently-priced shampoos.

3 I washed my hair in each shampoo for 2 minutes: to ensure that each shampoo was treated the same; or to ensure that the length of washing did not interfere with my results.

4 Other factors that could be controlled: volume of shampoo; how hard I pulled the comb; amount of rinsing; heat of the water; etc.

5 11.625

6 Completed graph:

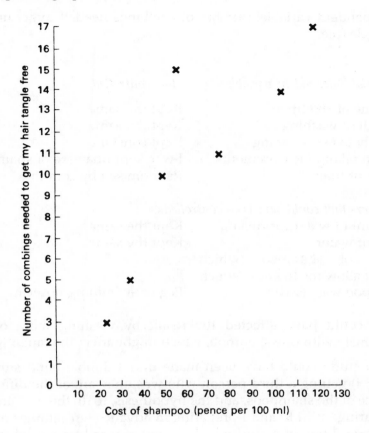

Cost of shampoo (pence per 100 ml)

7 Score that goes against the trend: the score for day 6 does not follow the trend of the more expensive the shampoo, the more combings needed.

8 The majority of scores follow the general trend that would be expected if my hypothesis was correct. Generally the more expensive the shampoo the more combings are needed.

Page 15

1 General format of a hypothesis:

A change in the independent variable will affect the dependent variable.

2 Independent variable: type of shampoo, expensive or cheap.

Dependent variable: number of combings needed to get my hair tangle free.

3

Potential independent variables	How controlled
Volume of shampoo	Kept the same
Length of washing	Kept the same
Time between washing	Kept constant
Bias in taking measurements	I was kept unaware of shampoo
Order of trials	Randomised by coin toss

4 *Others that could have been controlled:*

Amount of water for rinsing	Kept the same
Heat of water	Kept the same
Smell of shampoo (which would allow me to know which shampoo was used)	Peg or swimming noseclip

5a Jo could have affected the result by washing more or less vigorously with one shampoo, which might affect the tangling.

b The study could have been made into a double blind study by either: i) getting a third person who was unaware of the difference in price of the shampoos, and the hypothesis, to do the washing and measuring; or ii) Jo and I preparing in advance ten samples of each shampoo. I would record which shampoo was being used, and Jo would wash my hair with her eyes shut and nose clipped and then comb my hair. At the end we could match up the records of the shampoo used with the number of combings.

Pages 17–18

1 Completed table:

	Mean	Mode	Median
Cheap shampoo	9.5	9	9
Expensive shampoo	11.14	11	11

2 Range of combings for expensive shampoo: 8

3 Completed histogram for the results of the expensive shampoo:

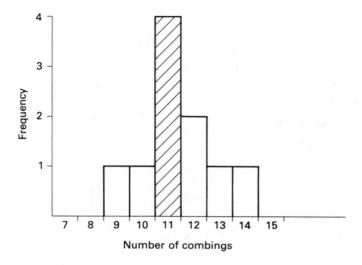

Number of combings

4 The answer should indicate that the averages are all higher for the expensive shampoo; if the histograms are compared the majority of results for the cheap shampoo are at a lower level than the expensive shampoo.

5 Trial 7 with the cheap shampoo produced the highest number of combings. This goes against the general trend of the results.

Pages 19–20

1a This question has no definite answer apart from: no matter how many times you toss the coins you could never be 100% sure that you had picked the right coin. Even a properly-weighted coin could by chance continue to land head up, or by chance continue to land tails up. So the answer to **b** must be: No.

c and d The chances of getting the corrrect answer increase the more times that the coins are tossed. The more times the coins are tossed the more the chance of getting the wrong answer are decreased. So if you value your life you would want to toss the coins as many times as possible.

2 Completion of the table and graph:

2	1+1	1
3	1+2,2+1	2
4	2+2,1+3,3+1	3
5	2+3,3+2,1+4,4+1	4
6	3+3,2+4,4+2,5+1,1+5	5
7	3+4,4+3,5+2,2+5,6+1,1+6	6
8	4+4,5+3,3+5,6+2,2+6	5
9	5+4,4+5,6+3,3+6	4
10	5+5,6+4,4+6	3
11	5+6,6+5	2
12	6+6	1

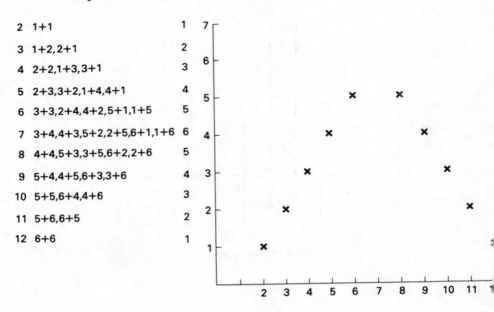

a Least likely total: Either 2 or 12

b Most likely total: 7

c Total number of outcomes: 36 (NB 6 × 6)

d 1 in 36

NB Notice the similarity in the shape between the table and the graph. It took me years to realise that when a line is drawn on a frequency distribution, the area below it represented scores, and the area above it was empty. (I thought the line was just hanging in mid-air!) Someone simply forgot to tell me.

Pages 22–3

1 The chance of winning the pools is less than one in ten million.

2
$p < 0.05$ = the probability is less than one in 20
$p < 0.002$ = the probability is less than one in 500
$p < 0.01$ = the probability is less than one in 100
$p < 0.001$ = the probability is less than one in 1000

3

$p < 0.99$ = the probability is less than 99 out of 100
$p > 0.99$ = the probability is greater than 99 out of 100
$p > 0.9$ = the probability is greater than 9 out of 10
$p > 0.995$ = the probability is greater than 199 out of 200

4

$p = 0.05$ = 5%
$p = 0.005$ = 0.5%
$p = 0.9995$ = 99.95%

Pages 24–5

1a Independent variable: Amount of alcohol

b Dependent variable: Score on Space Invader machine

c Null hypothesis: The amount of alcohol a person has will cause no difference in their score on a Space Invader machine

2

Significance level	Level of confidence
$p < 0.1$	$p > 0.9$, or greater than 90%
$p < 0.002$	$p > 0.998$, or greater than 99.8%
$p < 0.0001$	$p > 0.9999$, or greater than 99.99%

3 Areas of research needing higher levels of confidence: medical research, weapons research.

4 Reasons for needing higher levels of confidence: If the results of the research are going to be applied in a way in which the consequences of being wrong could be disastrous, eg if manufacturers are marketing a new drug they need to be really sure that there are no dangerous or lethal side-effects.

5 If the independent variable affects the dependent variable this is called an *experimental effect*.

6 The aim of any experiment is not to prove the hypothesis but to try to *test* or *falsify* the null hypothesis.

If a test tells an experimenter that there is not a significant difference the experimenter must *accept* the null hypothesis. If there is a significant difference they must *reject* the null hypothesis and *accept* the experimental hypothesis.

NB Null hypotheses are either rejected or accepted on the basis of statistical tests, but the experimental hypothesis can only be accepted. It is not correct to talk about the experimental hypothesis being rejected because the aim of the experiment is to test the null hypothesis.

Page 27

Completed table

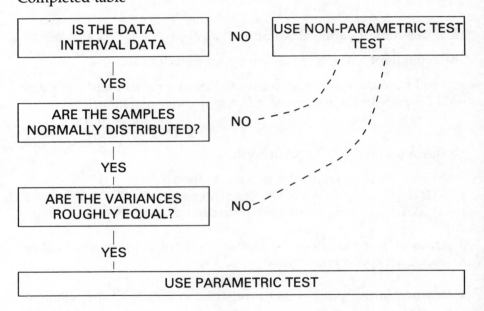

IS THE DATA INTERVAL DATA — NO → USE NON-PARAMETRIC TEST TEST

YES

ARE THE SAMPLES NORMALLY DISTRIBUTED? — NO

YES

ARE THE VARIANCES ROUGHLY EQUAL? — NO

YES

USE PARAMETRIC TEST

Page 30

1					2			
Trial	Set A	Set B	Sign		Trial	Set C	Set D	Sign
1	10	9	−		1	8	9	+
2	11	8	−		2	10	9	−
3	10	11	+		3	11	12	+
4	11	10	−		4	10	12	+
5	9	10	+		5	11	12	+
6	10	9	−		6	10	13	+
7	11	8	−		7	8	10	+
8	12	10	−		8	11	12	+
9	10	9	−		9	12	13	+
					10	9	10	+
					11	10	11	+
					12	9	12	+

$T = 9$
$L = 2$
Table value = 0.180
With a $p < 0.05$ significance
level the null hypothesis would
be: Accepted

$T = 12$
$L = 1$
Table value = 0.006
With a $p < 0.01$ significance
level the null hypothesis would
be: Rejected

3 The confidence level for 2) is $p > 0.99$.

Page 31

The second and fourth hypotheses are one-tailed.

Page 33

1 The claims that I made that cannot definitely be supported by the experiment were:

a That we had found 'definite proof' of a tangling agent in shampoos. The word 'proof' should be avoided.

b That the chemical companies are putting the agent in for the purpose of tangling the hair.

c That all expensive shampoos would cause more tangling.

d That the results from my hair generalised to everyone else. People with hair of a different type may react differently.

2 Measures of arithmetical ability:

a Results in an English exam: this would be an invalid measure as a person's ability in English is not necessarily related to their arithmetical ability.

b How neatly they write numbers: although an extreme of scruffyness might hamper a person's arithmetical ability this also is an invalid measure.

c Number of times they use a calculator in a Maths exam: I would also say that this is invalid as a person may have very good arithmetical abilities but use the calculator to make sure.

d Speed of solving arithmetical problems: valid.

3 Completed paragraph:

The *reliability* of a measure refers to whether it can be taken consistently. If I measure the size of a person's head with a tape measure, and each time I measure it I get the same result, this means my measure is *reliable*. I would be a fool to say that this was a *valid* measure of their intelligence, as intelligence is not related to the size of a person's head. The *validity* of a measure refers to whether it measures what the experimenter says it does.

Page 35

1a Independent variable: amount of alcohol drunk

   b Dependent variable: score on Space Invader machine

   c Conditions or levels of independent variables: no alcohol/three pints of beer.

   d If there is no difference in the results this could be explained by either: i) all of one group being Space Invader experts so that their scores when under the influence of three pints of beer are the same as the other group of non-experts when sober; ii) all of the alcohol group being heavy drinkers so that their performance is not very much affected by the three pints; iii) performance on space invaders is not affected by alcohol in the same way as other tests of motor performance.

Pages 37–8

1 The matched groups design is a more sensitive design than the independent groups design because it avoids *inter-subject variability*.

2 Completed graph:

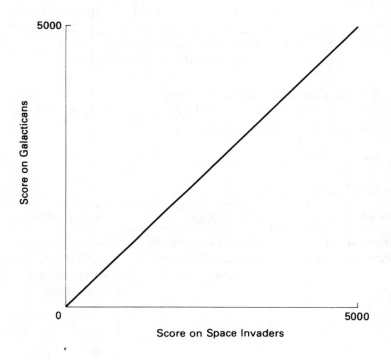

3 Researchers sometimes prefer to match subjects on a measure that predicts performance on the dependent variable to avoid the subjects having practice on the dependent variable itself before the experiment starts.

4 Matched groups:

GROUP 1	GROUP 2
S1	S4
S2	S7
S3	S13
S5	S14
S8	S9

Page 39

1 Completed diagram:

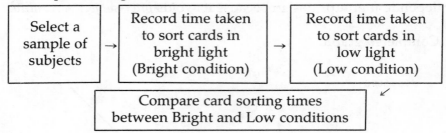

2 In the alcohol and Space Invader experiment, if the alcohol condition was first there would have to be a long period between conditions for the subject to sober up.

Page 40

Completed table

Type of design	Advantages	Disadvantages
Independent groups design	Results cannot be confounded by order effects	Results can be confounded by inter-subject variability Is uneconomical as it only uses each subject once
Matched groups design	Results cannot be confounded by order effects Results cannot be confounded by inter-subject variability	Is uneconomical as it only uses each subject once, and subjects have to be discarded
Repeated measures design	Results cannot be confounded by inter-subject variability Is economical as it uses subjects more than once	Results can be confounded by order effects

Pages 42–3

1 Example Y is not counterbalanced.

2 X and Z are counterbalanced *across* subjects.

3 Counterbalancing within conditions and across subjects. Half the subjects do the ABBA order, and half do BAAB.

4a Counterbalancing cannot balance out knowledge effects, large practice effects or asymmetrical combinations of effects.

b Counterbalancing can only balance out small order effects. This does not get rid of the effects, it spreads the effects between conditions so that hopefully they do not affect the results.

Page 45

1 Completed table

	Advantages	Disadvantages
Mean	1 Uses all the scores 2 Uses all the values of the scores	1 Is affected by extreme scores 2 Is not always an actual score
Median	1 Uses all the scores 2 Is not affected by extreme scores	1 Is not a real score 50% of the time 2 Does not use the values of the scores
Mode	1 Is always an actual score 2 Is not affected by extreme scores	1 Does not use all the scores 2 Does not use the values of the scores

2a Discrete

b Continuous

c Discrete

d Discrete

Page 48

Completed table

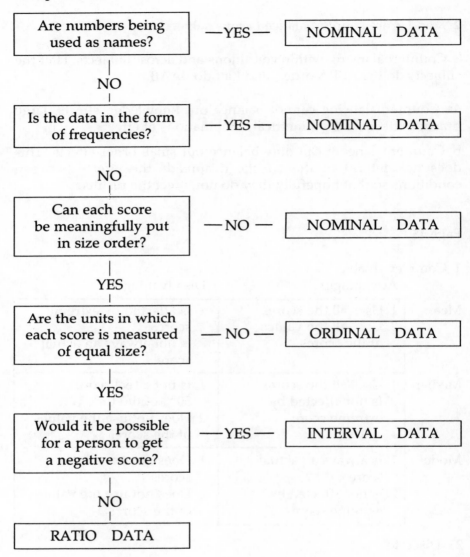

Which kind of data?

a Ratio – as a person cannot be a negative height.

b Ratio – as a person cannot hold a negative number of letters.

c Ordinal – almost all data from questionnaires is ordinal. The only exceptions are specially-constructed questionnaires such as those constructed using Thurstone's method of equal intervals and even then some statisticians believe that they should be treated as ordinal.

d Nominal – the numbers are being used as names of positions

e Ordinal

f Interval

Pages 49–50

1 Comparison of scores:

	Mean	Range
SET A	4	4
SET B	4	4

2 Completed frequency distributions:

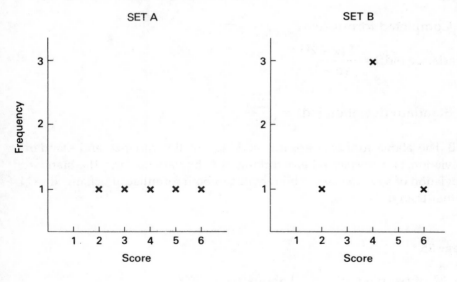

a The scores are on average closer to the mean in Set B.

b Set B has the smaller variance.

Page 51

1 Completed table for Set B:

A Score	B Mean score	C Difference between score and mean	D Difference squared	
2	4	−2	4	Number of scores = 5
4		0	0	
4		0	0	Number of scores minus one = 4
4		0	0	
6		2	4	Variance = 8 − 4 = 2
Total = 20			Total = 8	

2 Standard deviation for Set B: the square root of 2 = 1.41

Page 52

1 Completed formulae:

$$\text{Variance (sd}^2) = \frac{\Sigma(x - \bar{x})^2}{(n - 1)}$$

2 Standard deviation (sd) $= \sqrt{\dfrac{\Sigma(x - \bar{x})^2}{(n - 1)}}$

NB The above formulae are for working out the variance and standard deviation of a *sample*. When working out the variance and the standard deviation of a *population* the bottom line of both formulae are changed to N rather than n − 1.

Page 55

1a % of people with an IQ above 100 = 50%

b Probability of person picked at random from the population having an IQ over 100: p = 0.5

c % of people having an IQ between 100 and 120 = 34.2

d % of people having an IQ over 140 = 2%

188

e % of people having an IQ over 60 = 98%

f % of people having an IQ between 60 and 80 = 13.8%

g Probability of person picked at random from the population having an IQ less than 60 = 0.02%

h Most likely simple mean = 100

i Most probable mean IQ = 100. As there are more people with an IQ of 100 than any other score this means that people with an IQ of 100 are the most likely to be picked out at random. As scores get higher or lower than 100 the number of people with that score decreases and so their probability of being picked decreases.

Pages 57–8

1 Completed paragraph:

When designing an experiment we try to keep everything constant in each condition to avoid the effects of *constant* errors. Even if we control everything that we can think of, there is still the possibility that there are small uncontrollable variables that are *random* errors. If we use the matched subjects design or the repeated measures design we can control for *inter*-subject variability, but we can never control for *intra*-subject variability. In the repeated measures design there is the possibility of order effects which will introduce *constant* errors, but these can be minimised through *counterbalancing* or *randomisation*. The results of an independent groups design are likely to differ *more* than the results of matched subject or repeated measures designs because of *random* errors.

2 Completed table:

	Parametric test	Non-parametric test
Independent groups design	*Independent* t test	Mann-Whitney U test
Matched subjects or repeated measures	*Correlated* t test	Wilcoxon test or Sign test

NB To help remember which non-parametric test goes with which design remember that the one that sounds like an independent brewery goes with the independent groups design.

Page 60

1a Scattergram 1 = a negative correlation

b Scattergram 1 = a zero correlation

c Scattergram 1 = a positive correlation

2 When there is a positive correlation, as measurements of one variable increase, the measurements of the other variable tend to increase.

When there is a negative correlation, as measurements of one variable increase the measurements of the other variable tend to decrease.

When there is no relationship between the measurements of two variables it is called a zero correlation.

Page 62

1 Completed scattergram:

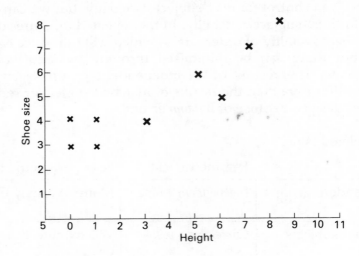

2a Negative correlation between distance of Haleys comet from earth and the price of petrol. I would guess that this was a chance correlation as I cannot think of any possible third variables and as I do not believe in astrology I think a causal explanation is very unlikely.

190

b Positive correlation between the size of a person's house and the size of their car. I would guess that this is likely to be explained by a third variable, eg a person's income: larger houses are more expensive and so are larger cars; or size of family, both need a lot of space; or size of person . . . or a combination of similar third variables.

c Negative correlation between effectiveness of memory and the amount of revision needed to pass exams. I would guess that this could be causal as exams rely upon memory, or it could be a third variable such as general intelligence (if such a quality exists).

The above explanations are just guesses and strictly correlations should be treated as just correlations with all three explanations being equally likely until there is evidence to suggest that one explanation is more likely than the others.

Pages 63–4

1 This will be dependent on your group.

2 This will be dependent on your group.

3 This is also dependent on your group, but a possible population is psychology students in further education.

Page 67

Crossword one

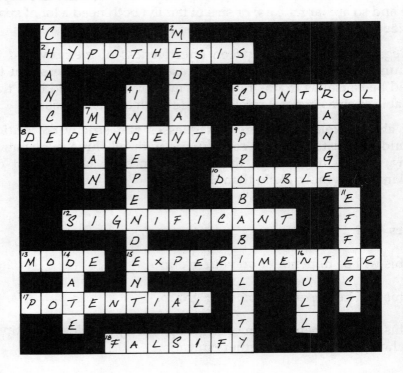

Crossword two

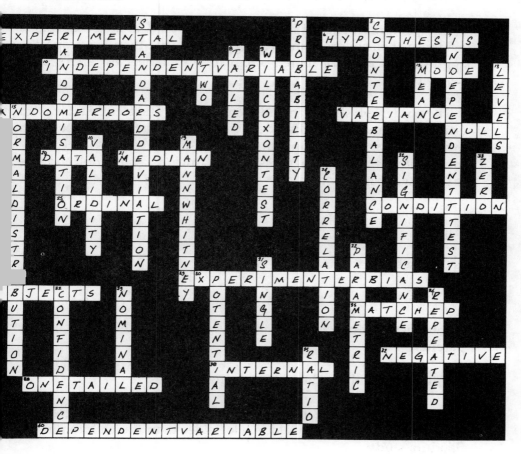

1 96 subjects were used.

2 Average age: 4 yrs 4 mths.

3 Experimental conditions: Real-life adult model
Filmed adult model
Cartoon model
Control condition: No model.

4 Average total aggression and average imitation of aggression towards doll.

5 The group that saw a cartoon model.

6 The group that saw a real-life adult model.

7 The paragraph should include reference to: The idea that this is evidence that children imitate aggression; that they learn specific aggressive acts; that filmed and cartoon models do affect their behaviour.

8 The paragraph should include reference to: The fact that it was an artificial situation; how often does a child watch a film and get put in exactly the same situation?; that the real-life model resulted in the most imitation; that the aggression was towards a bobo doll and this is in no way anti-social.

Page 78

1 One subject

2 15 years old

3 Interviews by psychiatrists and psychologists with Ronald and his parents.

4 Interviews with teachers; friends; neighbours.

5 The evidence relates to a real-life situation, with real aggression against a real person. Ronald is a lot older than the children in the Bandura study.

6 The paragraph should include reference to: only one subject and therefore the results cannot be generalised; the evidence is collected after the fact and this may cause the parents to remember only those things that fit in with the story; Ronald reported that TV had not taught him to kill anybody, and did not himself blame TV; the other evidence suggests that he was violent anyway.

7 The paragraph should include reference to the fact that a real person was killed. Although it is difficult to claim a cause and effect relationship between television and the murder there is evidence that Ronald's thinking was influenced by TV in that he likened the situation to TV; the TV may have given him a distorted view of reality.

194

1 85

2 Answer should include reference to: the control over viewing habits; the control over other daytime behaviours; and the ability to directly observe. All of which would be limited or at least difficult to gain in a housing estate.

3 The answer should include reference to: more natural surroundings; more representative sample.

4 The HA group who saw the violent films.

5 The paragraph should include reference to the fact that it was an abnormal population; in an abnormal situation it is very rare that you get such large groups watching TV together and this may have contributed to the effect; the boys were couped up inside an institution and perhaps they did not have enough space to work out their frustrations.

6 The paragraph should include reference to the fact that the aggressive films were associated with an increase in violence; that the effects were long lasting; the increases in violence occurred in an everyday setting for these boys.

Pages 82–3

1 427

2 The mothers were asked to name the children's three favourite programmes and these were then rated as violent or non-violent.

3 By asking the teenagers directly what their three favourite programmes were.

4 Answer should indicate that: peers have knowledge of how a person acts both in the presence of adults, and out of sight of adults.

5 Preference for violent TV age 8–9 and peer-rated aggression age 8–9: relationship.

Preference for violent TV age 18–19 and peer-rated aggression age 8–9: no relationship.

Preference for violent TV age 18–19 and peer-rated aggression age 18–19: no relationship.

Preference for violent TV age 8–9 and peer-rated aggression age 18–19: relationship.

6 Answer should include reference to the fact that this is correlational evidence and there are three possible explanations; it could be that aggressive children like aggressive TV; there could be other personality factors, or family factors (third variables).

7 Answer could include reference to Bandura study demonstrating that violent TV can lead to an increase in aggression; the case study showing that real-life violence may be linked to watching of violent TV; the possibility from Eron's study that viewing violent TV at an early age causes the child to become aggressive at that age and because of this develop an aggressive personality.

Pages 84–5

1 Age of subjects: 7–9 years

2 Completed graph:

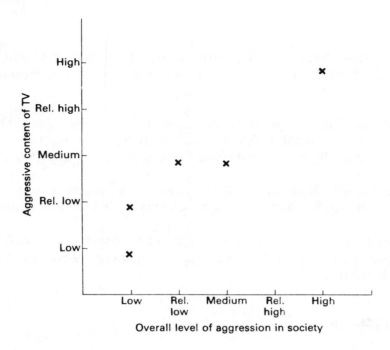

Overall level of aggression in society

3 It is a positive correlation.

4 The paragraph should include reference to many uncontrolled factors; the findings are also correlational and we cannot conclude that there is necessarily a cause and effect relationship; the finding that aggressive TV had no effect on children in the kibbutz; the way the societies are organised. If parents and teachers stressed co-operation more then we would have less aggressive societies.

5 The paragraph should include reference to: strong correlations between the level of violence that 7 to 9-year-olds view and their level of aggression; overall relationship between the amount of aggression shown on TV and the amount of aggression in society.

Page 87

1 Introduction of TV: presence or absence of TV

2 Crime rates

3 Group B

4 Group A

5 To ensure that it was the introduction of TV that increased the level of crime and not other changes that happened during one of the time periods.

6 Criminal statistics: people only report crimes if they think there is some chance that the police will act on them; some reports to the police, especially for domestic incidents, may not be recorded, etc.

7 The paragraph should include reference to: no increase in violence; real-life situation; large samples making it a reliable finding.

8 The paragraph should include reference to: lower level of violence in 1950s; only uses levels of reported crime; more realistic portrayal of violence these days.

Pages 144–146

Answers to reasoning problems:

Set 1 1 VALID, 2 VALID, 3 INVALID, 4 INVALID
Set 2 1 INVALID, 2 INVALID, 3 VALID, 4 VALID

Explanation of reasoning problems:

There are basically two forms of the reasoning problems that are valid.

1 DENYING THE CONSEQUENT (ie the 'then' bit): eg If p then q; not q, then not p.

2 AFFIRMING THE ANTECEDENT (ie the 'if' bit): eg If p then q; p, then q.

The other forms of denying the antecedent, and affirming the consequent are both logically invalid arguments.

198

The fact that these two forms are invalid becomes a little more obvious if the following examples are used:

DENYING ANTECEDENT

If human then two legs
Not human ——————— These do not follow as other animals
Therefore not two legs   can have two legs

AFFIRMING CONSEQUENT

If human then two legs
Two legs
Therefore human

NB A good discussion of logical reasoning and the problems most people have with it can be found in Chapter Five of: Sanford AJ (1987) *The Mind of Man*, Harvester Press.

Answers to questions on probability

1 Blue

2 Yellow

3 Either

4 22

Summary chart

Complete the table below as a summary of the advantages and disadvantages of methods of investigation in psychology

	Advantages	Disadvantages
Laboratory experiments		
Case studies		
Longitudinal studies		
Field studies		
Natural experiments		
Cross cultural studies		